REISS
DAIRY

Stephen Reiss

AuthorHouse™
1663 Liberty Drive
Bloomington, IN 47403
www.authorhouse.com
Phone: 1 (833) 262-8899

Because of the dynamic nature of the Internet, any web addresses or links contained in this book may have changed
since publication and may no longer be valid. The views expressed in this work are solely those of the author and do
not necessarily reflect the views of the publisher, and the publisher hereby disclaims any responsibility for them.

Any people depicted in stock imagery provided by Getty Images are models,
and such images are being used for illustrative purposes only.
Certain stock imagery © Getty Images.

This book is printed on acid-free paper.

ISBN: 978-1-7283-7281-5 (sc)
ISBN: 978-1-7283-7282-2 (e)

Library of Congress Control Number: 2020917012

Print information available on the last page.

Published by AuthorHouse 09/18/2020

authorHOUSE®

Contents

Introduction Number One

"Standard Democrat" October 27, 2003
Reiss Dairy History as Told by Lonnie Standley

John Jacob Reiss founded the Reiss Dairy in Sikeston, Missouri. He started selling milk from his own cows to neighbors and then to local retailers. That led to starting his own dairy and becoming a retailer himself. "About the year 1940, when Reiss Dairy was located in a frame building at 523 East Malone Avenue in Sikeston, processed milk products were packaged in glass – that is all products except butter which was packaged in folded cardboard one-pound cartons."

"Reiss Diary packaged processed milk in three sizes of cartons – ½ pint, pint, and quart sizes. The bottles were purchased in shipments when needed by the truckloads from glass bottle manufacturers. I can remember only two manufacturers – Owens-Illinois Glass and Liberty Glass Co. All manufacturers would apply sizes and the Dairy trade name on the bottle. We selected red as the color of this application. The name was more or less permanent, depending on the caustic washing material used and the wear and tear of constant use. One of the manufacturers told us we could place an advertising message on the opposite side of the bottle so here is where the applied verses began."

"We decided we would ask our customers to help us advertise Reiss Dairy products. We placed a paid advertisement in the twice a week Sikeston Standard. We placed this advertisement only once at a probable cost of less than $10. The size of the advertisement was two columns by eight included for the single insertion. The advertisement read something like this: Do you like to doodle or write ditties? Write your choice and bring it to the Reiss Dairy Office. When you see your work placed on a Reiss Dairy Milk Bottle, bring the bottle to our Reiss Dairy Office and collect $1.00 cash. Reiss Dairy 523 East Malone Avenue, Sikeston, Missouri."

"This advertisement brought very slow results, but gradually interest increased and poems came in – in large numbers. As we placed orders for new bottles, the poems were changed and new poems were selected. We kept this program in effect until we changed milk packaging from glass to paper which was in 1949 when we were in our new building at 526 S. Main Street in Sikeston."

"I have no idea how many verses we received, but the ladies working in our office really enjoyed making the selections of verses when new orders for milk bottles were placed. They placed all verses as received in a big box and stored in a safe place. When we began packaging milk in paper, we had milk bottles to destroy. We hauled milk bottles to the trash heap – truckloads of them. One lady told us that Reiss Dairy milk bottles are now valued at $150 on the Internet.

Introduction Number Two

Here's part of a story I wrote eight years ago to our (then) two young grandchildren about the Reiss Dairy. Now we have four grandchildren and the last two are Ava and Blake. All four are sweet kids, ages 5, 6, 8, and 10. I had resolved on Palm Sunday 2012 to write two stories every Monday to our grands because I was already 65 years old than them and realized that we would never have many heavy adult conversations. Writing Granddad's Mondays stories every Monday was my only option to make sure family history, fun times, philosophies, etc. would survive me. My 1,000[th] Granddad's Mondays story went on May 11, 2020. Every December, stories for that year are bound into Christmas books for each grand, their parents, and ourselves.

Reiss Dairy

Dear Will and Kayla,   October 15, 2012

You may not remember this but shortly after each of you was born and your moms were supplying all your milk, each referred to themselves as "The Reiss Dairy." Pretty clever, don't you think? But it was 74 years ago this past Saturday on October 13, 1938 that the following advertisement appeared in "The Sikeston (Missouri) Herald" newspaper that eventually made the original Reiss Dairy very famous. Here's the history.

Sikeston is located just north of the boot-heel of southeast Missouri or about halfway between St. Louis and Memphis. The city was founded in 1860 and named for John Sikes. Current population is 16,500.

Are You A DITTLER or a DOODLER?

In case you don't already know, a dittler is a writer of ditties, and a doodler is a person who, during spare time, draws objects of art, geometric figures, artistic representations, etc.

You may wonder where lies the connection between Reiss Dairy and Dittlers and Doodlers— Here it is:

Reiss Dairy will pay $1.00 each for ditties to be put on the reverse side of our milk bottles. You are already acquainted with Old King Cole, Yankee Doodle, Little Miss Muffett and others.

Write your ditty on a sheet of paper and you may accompany it with a suitable doodle (drawing) if you wish, then hand same to a Reiss Dairy salesman or mail direct to ReissDairy.

The best ditties and doodles will be put on the reverse side of Reiss Dairy milk bottles with the name of the author below.

REISS DAIRY

In 1926 your great great great uncle John Reiss started his own dairy business on his farm just northeast of Sikeston. He was milking 10 cows and called his business Reiss Dairy Farm. His milk bottles had raised or embossed letters and were not painted. He bottled and sold milk from other farmers as his business grew.

In 1935 he built a new processing building in Sikeston, brought his son-in-law Lonnie Standley into the business, and renamed it Reiss Dairy. They soon changed away from embossed milk bottles to smooth painted or pyroglaze milk bottles. At different times over the next two decades they also sold ice cream, dairy bars, eggs, whipping cream, cottage cheese, and related items. They had a lunch counter called the Cow Bell where sundaes and other treats were created for customers. I remember  enjoying a marshmallow sundae at this counter in August 1961, and it was free! They chose Jo-Kay as the name for their ice cream after Lonnie's two daughters, Jo Ellen and Kay. Neat idea, don't you think? It would be like naming our home-made applesauce Will-Kay after the two of you.

Love, Granddad

Dedication

My second cousin Katy Standley supplied much of history and inspiration for this book about her father Lonnie Standley, grandfather John "Papa" Reiss, their wives, and the unique Reiss Dairy business they created in Sikeston, Missouri. Katy also supplied most of the photographs and letters. Without her significant help, the first and second editions of this book would not have been possible.

Katy also arranged for my presentation and book-signing of first edition to be part of the 50th reunion weekend of her class from Sikeston High School in 2011. That gathering was held at the former Sikeston Railroad Station which is now the Depot Museum. We sold 27 books to folks from Missouri, Ohio, Florida, Illinois, Arizona, Louisiana, North Carolina, Indiana, and Pennsylvania.

I should also mention that Katy is the proud mother of Arthur Bradley Soule IV, born 8/10/1980. On his father's side, his great grandfather's great grandfather is George Soule who sailed on the Mayflower to arrive at the Plymouth Colony in 1620 and who also signed the Mayflower Compact. On his mother's side, his ancestors landed at the Jamestown Colony about the same time. Brad was an officer in the US Coast Guard for many years and is now with Interpol in England.

Thank you very much, Katy. I shall be forever grateful. Thus, it gives me great pleasure to dedicate this second edition of **Reiss Dairy, Famous for Milk Bottles with Poems** to you, especially now that you are the matriarch of your branch of the extended Reiss Family.

Thanks, Katy!!!

Love, Steve

Dear Steve,

I hope you are pleased with this surprise — I think this is a quilt made by Aunt Katie for my grandmother, Mary Etta. I found it in a stack of old quilts. I remember it on Mama's bed. She was a wonderful seamstress but did not quilt. It obviously was much loved and well used. My mother kept it because it was a "family" quilt and because it was on Mama's bed when she died. So I hope you are pleased. You asked about your grandmother giving a quilt to her grandmother and I think this is it. I have not cleaned it — too fragile.

Love, Katy

PS: I'm showing our four young grandchildren, ages 5 to 10, as co-authors of this second edition because documenting family histories for all generations has been a huge part of my retirement years. They are my motivation. As authors, it will look good on their future resumes and should get them hits on Google, Amazon, Barns & Noble, etc.!!!

Thanks, Will, Kayla, Ava, and Blake.

Love, Granddad

Company History by Lonnie Standley
20 Years of Progress with Reiss Dairy

As to the history of the Reiss Dairy organization it is not an old company, but was started by John J. Reiss on his farm two miles east of Sikeston. The beginning of this enterprise was small indeed – a few quarts of milk delivered daily to homes and businesses in Sikeston. Reiss Dairy can count among its customers of fifteen years or longer many of the leading families of Sikeston. In 1935, Mr. Reiss decided that to more adequately serve the people of this area additional plant facilities were necessary, so he remodeled and added to a restaurant building at 523 E. Malone Avenue in Sikeston. In the meantime, the dairy had grown to a production of about 100 gallons each day. Various dairy products besides milk were being processed such as cottage cheese, butter, buttermilk, chocolate milk, etc. Reiss Dairy was the first dairy in the Sikeston area to process and sell pasteurized milk. The dairy plant on Malone Avenue in Sikeston has been remodeled and enlarged several times to take care of increasing business. At one time Reiss Dairy was serving six C.C.C. Camps in this area. Delivery routes were extended until today Reiss Dairy milk can be purchased in cities as far away as Chaffee, Caruthersville, East Prairie, and Gray Ridge.

The vision of Mr. Reiss and L. M. Standley, who came with the firm in 1935, has always been to approach the highest quality dairy product it is possible to produce. Plant facilities at the Malone Avenue plant were becoming crowded by the end of World War II. It was necessary to enlarge the plant or build a new one. After a lot of study and investigation the latter plan was decided upon. Ample land was purchased and plans were immediately started on a plant building not surpassed in quality and convenience by any dairy, anywhere. Dozens of drawings were made and finally with the assistance of dairy engineers everywhere, and competent architect the plans for the new Reiss Dairy Plant took shape. The plant layout is the simplest possible, the convenience for processing milk and the comfort of the employees was uppermost in the minds of the planners. The final plans also embraced the idea of a milk bar where the dairy would undertake to serve dairy products to the public in the proper manner. All this took place two years or more ago. Late in 1947 the contract was let for the construction of the new Reiss Dairy. Unavoidable delays slowed construction until almost a year later the milk bar (Cow Bell) was opened to the public.

You, our visitors and friends, are seeing today one of the finest dairy plants in Missouri. It is not fancy or elaborate, but no expense was spared, either in the building or equipment, to bring to the people of Southeast Missouri, the finest and best we could buy. We leave to your good judgment the decision as to whether Reiss Dairy did the right thing in providing for you and its other customers, a plant that has no superior anywhere. And remember this one thing, Reiss Dairy was never asked or coerced by any City Council or Health Department anywhere to make this investment for you. We appreciate your interest in Your Reiss Dairy, and we hope to merit your friendship for years to come.

"Two quarts of milk, please" you tell the milkman or grocer without giving a thought to how the milk gets to your door or to the store ready for you to take home. The story of milk's daily arrival, fresh and sweet, from farms often several miles from Sikeston is one of the fascinating stories of dairy development for better living. Dairying today is a modernized industry requiring many skilled workmen.

We realize the magnitude of the dairy industry as we learn that one out of fifteen families in the United States is dependent on dairying for a livelihood. Dairying is an industry carried on in each of the forty-eight states but the greatest dairy region is the Middle West and Pacific coast areas. There are about twenty-five million milk cows in the United States. The principle dairy breeds are the Holstein, Jersey and Guernsey. The demands of the market and climatic conditions are important factors in the selection of breeds of dairy cattle.

Dairy specialists in the United States Department of Agriculture report that about four acres of farm land, including two acres of pastures are needed to provide a year's food for a cow. The average cow gives six quarts of milk a day, but by selective breeding this production may reach ten, twelve or more quarts per day. The record production per cow for one year is about 42,000 pounds (about 19,500 quarts) of milk. In one year, an average dairy cow weighing 1,000 pounds will eat, in addition to pasturage, 6,300 pounds of silage, 2,700 pounds of alfalfa hay, and 1,700 pounds of grain. She drinks about eight gallons of water each day. In that time, she will produce about 900 gallons of milk.

The modern dairy farm is a scientifically planned enterprise. It consists of three main buildings, besides the homestead, and plenty of pasture land for the cows. The three main buildings are the barn, silo, and milk house. The size and arrangement of these buildings are varied to suit the dairyman, but essentially, they meet the requirements of the U. S. Public Health Code. The modern dairy barn is a clean, food producing plant. It has concrete floors, smooth walls and ceilings and stall partitions for the cows. Modern dairy barns are roomy with wide aisles for feeding and cleaning. Ample windows let in light, and ventilators help make the barn, dry, airy, and sanitary. Regular painting or whitewashing of the interior is a part of the schedule. Silage is grass, legumes or other crops chopped by machine and stored for winter use to provide green feed. Grains such as corn, oats, cottonseed or soybean meals provide the concentrated food. The milk house is a separate building (it may be attached to the barn) where the milk is cared for and cooled, before it is sent to the dairy. This building houses the equipment and utensils for milking, a mechanical milk cooler, and equipment for keeping utensils and the building clean. Milking may be done by hand or machine, but over 75% of Reiss Dairy milk is machine milked. Dairy cows are milked at least twice a day, and each morning the Reiss Dairy truck comes by the dairy farm and picks up both night and morning milk, both of which have previously been cooled.

Upon reaching the Reiss Dairy Plant, the milk is immediately received by a licensed milk buyer. He samples, weighs and examines the milk for quality before the cans are emptied. This is the last time the milk is exposed to the air until you pour it from the bottle in your home. From the weighing tank, the milk is immediately pumped to a storage tank, being cooled to 40 degrees or below and clarified on the way. After several thousand pounds of milk are received to the insulated storage tank, the fully automatic pasteurization system is set in motion. The milk follows at the rate of 4,500 pounds per hour. By exchanging cold for heat the milk is raised to 162 degrees and held at that temperature for at least sixteen seconds. By regeneration and cooling medium (ice water) the milk is immediately cooled to 40 degrees or less and bottled. Upon being bottled the milk is stored in an insulated, refrigerated room (40 degrees or less) until the milk is loaded on the Reiss Dairy trucks to be delivered to your homes or your grocer.

Such is the cycle of getting your milk to you. Naturally there are other pieces of equipment that were omitted in the above description, such as the can washer which washes, sterilizes and dries all dairymen's cans before they are returned to the farm. Another large item of equipment is the homogenizer which is essentially a sanitary high-pressure pump. Another intricate machine is the Purepak paper packaging machine. It is an interesting sight to see. Knocked down (flat) paper cartons are shaped, paraffined, filled and sealed all in one operation. These paper packages are purchased by the car load from a paper plant in Louisiana.

Here is a Google Earth map showing the three Reiss Dairies in Sikeston. Two miles northeast of downtown is the original family farm which became the Reiss Dairy Farm and Peach Orchard. The second dairy was at 523 East Malone Street which was the original building and several additions buildings as the business grew. The third dairy was at 526 South Main Street. At left is the former train depot now called the Depot Museum at 116 West Malone Street.

Reiss Dairy Farm

This is John Reiss and his wife Etta Mary with their first daughter Lillian who was born on 11/25/1911. It was taken in 1913 in front of their home and dairy farm two miles northeast of Sikeston, Missouri. They were apparently renting this farm because they did not buy it until 3/29/1918 per the deed on the next page. John supplied milk to his neighbors and other bottlers before opening their first dairy here called Reiss Dairy Farm about 1935. Their first bottles were embossed rather than painted with those words like the pint and quart bottles which follow.

John, Lillian and Mary Reiss about 1913

Ethel Reichert and Matt
Reichert, (her husband
    To
John J. Reiss and Etta M.
Reiss, husband and wife.

WARRANTY DEED.
Book 78, Page 462.
Dated March 29th, 1918.
Filed December 30th, 1918.
Consideration $16,995.00.

GRANT, BARGAIN AND SELL, CONVEY AND CONFIRM, unto the said parties of the second part, their heirs and assigns, the following described lots, tracts err parcels of land, lying, being and situate in the County of Scott and State of Missouri, to-wit: All of the North-west quarter (NW 1/4) of Section Twenty-one (21) that lies North of the North line of the right-of-way of the St. Louis-Iron-Mountain and Southern Railway, amounting to 83.906 acres in Township Twenty-six (26) North, of Range Fourteen (14) East,(and other lands)

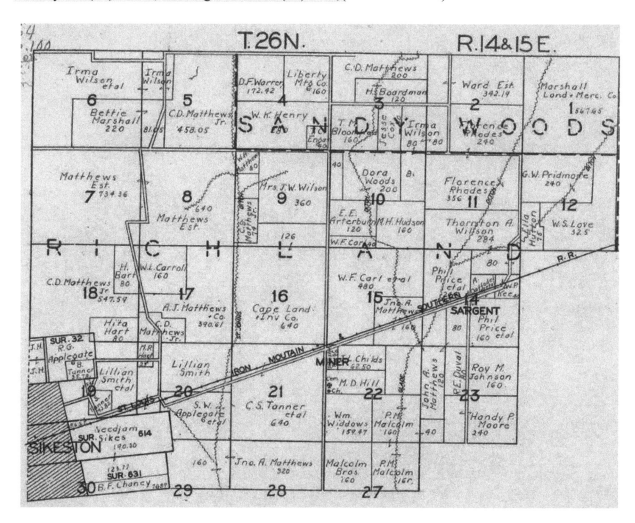

The Reiss farm is that triangle north of the railroad track in Section 21. This track and a depot in downtown Sikeston became operational on August 7, 1917. Shortly afterward, the depot and other facilities of the St. Louis and Iron Mountain Railroad were acquired by the Missouri Pacific Railroad. The Missouri Pacific continued operating the depot as the local passenger and freight station at Sikeston until October 15, 1985. It is now the very well-done Depot Museum.

John Reiss was the first driver delivering milk from his dairy. Here are his early pocket records from 1934.

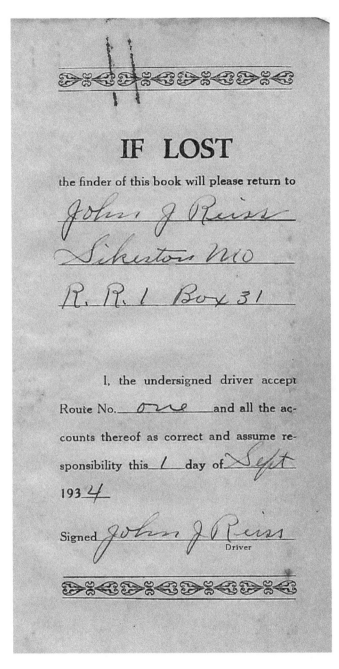

Here are John Reiss and daughter Lillian in front of their farm house 1922. His wife Etta Mary is driving the team of horses in front of the barn at right.

John Reiss planted 1,100 peach trees and developed that as a secondary business to milk.

Here's John with a bumper crop of peaches on August 28, 1922.

"The Sikeston Herald" – April 14, 1938
"Reiss Orchards in Excellent Condition"

The cold snap of last week which is said to have ruined a number of peach and apple orchards throughout Southeast Missouri, failed to reach the Reiss Orchards east of Sikeston, according to John J. Reiss, owner. The group of 1100 peach trees are heavily laden with fruit, some of which are as large small marbles. The small apple orchard was slightly damaged, it is thought, but not to any considerable extent.

"The Sikeston Herald" – June 13, 1940
Too Much Fruit on Reiss Trees

A "Believe It or Not" event took place at the John J. Reiss peach orchard east of Sikeston the past ten days when trees, too heavily laden with fruit, were reduced of their load by 50 per cent. "For the first time in the life of the orchard, we are picking peaches green," Mr. Reiss told a Herald reporter. "The crop is abundant and in order to allow the peaches to mature to their highest and best quality, the trees had to be relieved, so for the past ten days we have had a group of ten boys picking green peaches."

"Prospects for an excellent yield are exceedingly good, said Mr. Reiss, "and the prospect of good prices are equally as good. With only seven counties in Southeast Missouri surviving peach-killing cold, and with only small crops of peaches in the very tip of Southern Illinois, prices bid fair to reach from $2.00 to $2.50 per bushel and perhaps even higher." There are 1,000 trees of the J. H. Hale and the Early Elberta variety in the Reiss Orchard which is now eight years old. More than 4,000 bushels have been produced by the trees since they began to bear, with an average slightly more than $1.00 per bushel.

"The Sikeston Herald" August 29, 1940
"Reiss Orchards Yield 4500 Bushels Peaches"

From the thousand peach trees, of the Elberta and Hale varieties in the John Reiss Peach Orchard east of Sikeston, a yield of 4,500 bushels was realize upon completion of the harvest last week. Exactly two weeks were required to pick the fruit, which was of unusually good quality this season, with twenty men accomplishing the work. A large quantity of the peaches was sold locally and the remainder shipped to Ohio, Indiana, North Missouri, and Illinois.

"The Sikeston Herald" – August 19, 1942

The mercury stood at 52 degrees this week. And this is about the best news from a comfort standpoint that has happened in a week.

The Reiss Dairy Farm and Orchard, together with the dairy stock, were sold by Mr. and Mrs. John Reiss this week to P. J. Ponder of near Commerce.

John J. Reiss and Etta M.	WARRANTY DEED.
Reiss, husband and wife.	Book 134, Page 221.
To	Dated October 1st, 1943.
Philip J. Ponder, Jr.,	Filed October 1st, 1943.
And Evelyn Lankford Ponder	at 4:45 P. M.

GRANT, BARGAIN AND SELL, CONVEY AND CONFIRM, unto the said parties of the second part, their heirs and assigns, the following described lots, tracts or parcels of land, lying, being and situate in the County of Scott and State of Missouri, to-wit: All that part of the Northwest l/4 of Section 21 lying North of the North line of the right of way of the St. Louis, Iron Mountain and Southern Railway Company, all in Township 26 North, Range 14 East of the Fifth Principal Meridian.

On the next pages are two same-day 1932 farm-talk letters from Katherine and Alwin Gasser who both grew up a few miles from the Reiss family farm in St. Clair County, Illinois. They were married in 1919. They moved to Sikeston, Missouri in 1929 where they continued as friends of John and Mary Etta Reiss who founded the Reiss Dairy Farm. John was born on 11/4/1877 and Alwin on 8/7/1896 so they were a generation apart but the extended Gasser and Reiss families were probably church and Grange friends for decades in Illinois. Maybe the Gassers moved to Sikeston at the encouragement of John Reiss. The Gassers were farmers and raised grain to feed their chickens and beef/dairy cows. John Reiss was probably Alwin's customer for raw milk. All four are buried in Sikeston.

The 1930 Census shows Alwin age 33 and Katherine age 32 owning and operating a farm near Sikeston, Missouri. These two letters were sent to John Reiss' brother George and his wife Katie (my grandparents) who by then were owners of the Reiss family farm. It was their son Franklin who made a radio talk about his project on Rhode Island Red chickens. Franklin went on to a distinguished 43-year career as a professor of Agriculture at the University of Illinois.

Sikeston, Mo.
Mar. 6, 1932

Dear Friends,

Last nite we had the coldest nite this winter and also had snow yesterday all day. But none staid on the ground. Yesterday (Sat) noon we tuned in on the farm hour and of all surprises, we heard Franklin Reiss of Belleville announced to speak on his project. Yes, we heard him and he was the only one I understood every word. His was a very good talk and I don't know what to say that is right. But I guess congratulations would be a good word. It really made me feel homesick for good old Floraville. Franklin must be quite a man by now. I guess he's going to college now.

We get to see Mr. & Mrs. John Reiss quite often. They are doing very well and are having quite an up to date dairy business.

We did very well with our farming last year. But the low prices of all farm produce is hard on all farmers.

We passed your house last summer, when we were at home, but you were all gone. It was the Sunday Smithton Homecoming was held. We are wanting to visit home again, this summer if possible. We have a flock of about 140 hens, mostly S.C. Rhode Island Reds and they are a paying flock both as egg and as poultry. Eggs are to date 8 cents in trade at the stores. We ship all our cream to Sugar Creek Creamery. It keeps us two pretty busy all the year around, but we are both well and like to work.

Gilbert is with his uncle on a farm at Gulin, Mo. now. He went to St. Louis about a year ago. He's 22 years now. Will close hoping to hear from you soon.

As always your friend,
Katherine Gasser

Sikeston, Mo.
March 6, 1932

Dear Friends,

We heard Franklin talk about his "Reds" Saturday. His voice came thru better than any of the young men who have spoken this winter. With better farmers and their increased yields, our chemists will be kept busy finding new uses and new outlets for farm products.

We seeded oats last Tuesday and Wednesday. We raised last year 58 acres corn, 20 acres wheat, 26 oats, 15 closer, 30 soybeans after small grains for hay and seed and 12 acres permanent pasture. We are still following the cropping ideas we started with except that we added the beans and increased corn. Soys have been raised as a cash crop. In future we shall increase clover and raise soybeans as a grain crop only to be fed to stock. All of the hay and most of the grain is fed on the farm as you can see when I say that we raise and feed out annually about 25 hogs and have on hand 18 head of dairy cattle.

Last year we added a new line. We fed one steer. Total cost of raising and feeding it $15. Returns $35.67, net profit $20.67. We expect to feed more.

Most farms here are straight grain or grain & cotton farms. S. E. Missouri has the soil, the climate and markets to have a prosperous agriculture. It has too much of a one crop system. A bad financing system and large land-holdings. We are about 98% tenant farmers. Most of these have stock and equipment mortgaged and in addition annually mortgage their crops in advance to finance the year's operation. A bad policy. Share cropping is a good way for a beginner to get a start at farming but as used here is an agricultural drawback. We need farmers here who are willing to stand on their own feet, and able to see beyond the end of their nose.

You have doubtless read a bit about Korean Lespedeza lately. I seeded some on my permanent grass pasture two years ago. It is wonderful. You cannot imagine how good it really is when used in this connection unless you have tried it. It produces fine grazing from July until October and grass will come up just as green as every next spring.

Hoping that we may hear from our old neighbors now and then, I remain.

Yours,
Alwin G. Gasser

Reiss Dairy Newspaper Articles

"The Sikeston Herald" February 6, 1936

PROCESSING PLANT OF REISS DAIRY IS NEW INDUSTRY OF 1935

The Reiss Dairy was started nine years ago on the Reiss Farm 1.5 miles west of Sikeston. The growth of the business has been so rapid that during this time the owner and operator, J. J. Reiss has erected four new buildings.

The herd has increased from 10 cows to 50 at present, composed of Jersey and Holstein with Holstein predominating. This herd is tested regularly for tuberculosis and Bang's disease so as to keep the milk free from these disease germs.

In August 1935 the machinery was moved to the new plant erected on East Malone Avenue. This building contains the following rooms: office, refrigerating, pasteurizing and bottling, receiving, storeroom, bottle washing room and boiler room. The machinery includes a 100-pound butter churn, 100-gallon pasteurizer, 50-gallon cheese vat, 12-sample Babcock cream tester, two-bottle electric washer, three-compartment bottle-washing vat (soaking, rinsing and sterilizing) and a York ammonia ice machine.

The pasteurizing procedure carried out at the Reiss Dairy to ensure germ-free milk is as follows: The fresh whole milk is brought in from the farm shortly after it is milked. Before it is put into the pasteurizer it is strained through a cotton filter disc, which is removed and a new disc inserted for every 10 gallons of milk. In the pasteurizer, it is heated by steam to 142 degrees Fahrenheit where it is held for 30 minutes. This process kills all the bacteria harmful to human beings. At the end of 30 minutes an electric pump forces the milk over a cooler where the temperature is reduced to 36 degrees Fahrenheit. Brine from the ice machine is forced through the cooler while the milk is pouring over it. The milk runs into the bottle-filler where it is bottled and capped in one operation. Danger of contamination is very small because the whole system is taken apart, washed and sterilized after each batch is pasteurized, also the milk is never exposed to the air from the time it is put into the pasteurizer until the bottle is opened in the home. Surplus milk is made into buttermilk and cottage cheese.

The cream used in making butter is purchased from farmers in the vicinity of Sikeston. The cream is pasteurized by a process similar to that in pasteurizing milk and is churned in the Reiss plant. The farmers receive over $200 each week for cream bought by the Reiss Dairy. Most of the butter is sold locally but some of the milk goes to the United States CCC camps at Hayti and New Madrid.

"The Sikeston Herald" 1938 New Building Edition

During the past year, Reiss Dairy enlarged its plant on East Malone Avenue, adding a new storage room at the south of the original plant and enlarging the cold-storage room.

Several pieces of new equipment were added, providing for more modern production and delivery of the many dairy products sold by this firm. Two new delivery trucks were added to those already in use, making a total of five trucks operated by Reiss.

The dairy also purchased tow new 150-gallon stainless steel pasteurizers, a new 3500-pound churn and other smaller equipment during the past year. The refrigeration plant was re-arranged and the brine-spray system of cooling was installed.

Two new towns were added to those already served by the Reiss Dairy – Hayti and Chaffee. Practically all towns on the Reiss delivery routes are given daily service except Sikeston where products are delivered regularly twice each day.

The Reiss Dairy is planning further improvements in 1938 – both in the quality of its products and the service of its delivery system. Announcements of these improvements will be made in the near future.

"The Sikeston Herald" October 13, 1938
Advertisement – REISS DAIRY

Are You A
DITTLER or a DOODLER?

In case you don't already know, a dittler is a writer of ditties, and a doodler is a person who, during spare time, draws objects of art, geometric figures, artistic representations, etc.

You may wonder where lies the connection between Reiss Dairy and Dittlers and Doodlers—
Here it is:

Reiss Dairy will pay $1.00 each for ditties to be put on the reverse side of our milk bottles. You are already acquainted with Old King Cole, Yankee Doodle, Little Miss Muffett and others.

Write your ditty on a sheet of paper and you may accompany it with a suitable doodle (drawing) if you wish, then hand same to a Reiss Dairy salesman or mail direct to ReissDairy.

The best ditties and doodles will be put on the reverse side of Reiss Dairy milk bottles with the name of the author below.

REISS DAIRY

"The Sikeston Herald" October 20, 1938
"Dittlers and Doodlers Abound in Sikeston"

Seemingly a large number of Sikestonians answered "yes" to the question asked by the Reiss Dairy in last week's Herald – "Are You a Dittler or a Doodler?" Approximately 75 persons responded to the advertisement with suggested "ditties" and "doodles" to be put on the reverse side of Reiss Dairy milk bottles. The best ones submitted will be put on the bottles with the author's name below, and will also win the writer a prize of $1.00.

The contest will continue this week. Details are to be found in the advertisement of the Reiss Dairy published elsewhere in this issue of The Herald.

"The Sikeston Herald" December 1, 1938

Reiss Dairy Begins Use of Ditties and Sketches Submitted by Customers

The Reiss Dairy has this week begun to use a number of ditties and sketches submitted by customers and other citizens of the territory served by this enterprising business firm.

In response to an advertisement published exclusively by The Herald a few weeks ago, approximately 250 ditties concerning the use of milk were submitted and according to officials of the Dairy, ditties are still being presented. Also about fifty drawings of the objects and scenes suggestive of the proper use of milk were submitted. The preponderance of ditties over the drawings submitted indicated that most folks can write better than they can draw.

Of the many drawings and ditties submitted, five were etched onto the sides of 14,000 milk bottles received this week by the Dairy for use in Sikeston and the many other Southeast Missouri towns served by it. The etchings are in red making them very noticeable when the bottles are filled.

One group of bottles is etched with a ditty and drawing submitted by Carol Headlee, a 16-year-old high school girl of Morehouse. The drawing shows a football player in the act of making a touchdown. The ditty reads as follows:

> "Frail weak Tommy couldn't play,
> But to do so was his aim;
> He drank milk and now he's strong,
> And today he won the game."

Another ditty, above which is etched the "crooked man who walked a crooked mile" was submitted by Mrs. G. Poynor of Sikeston. It reads:

"There was a crooked man –
Who would have been quite straight,
If every day he'd found a glass
Of milk beside his plate."

A Sikeston businessman submitted this ditty:

"There was a man in our town
and he was wondrous wise.
For the only milk he would drink
Was REISS Pasteurized."

Mrs. J. L. Osborn submitted this ditty:

"Oh boy, what a joy
To feel as fine as silk;
Please get wise, open your eyes,
Use nothing but REISS' Milk."

"The Sikeston Herald" February 2, 1939
"Continued Expansion at Reiss Dairy"

More than $65,000 worth of raw milk was bought from farmers of this district by the Reiss Dairy during the past year, John J. Reiss, co-owner, stated this week. This milk was used in the manufacture of the approximate 700 gallons of pasteurized milk per day, as well as cheese, butter and other products of the dairy.

Seven hundred gallons of milk per day would equal 255,500 gallons for the year and, figured in the way most of us take our milk, that would be 1,022,000 quarts. Which is a lot of milk, no matter how you figure it.

In accordance with its practice of supplying the best dairy products possible, the Reiss Dairy this year has installed a number of new machines and equipment including a can washer, bottle washer, pasteurizer, cheese-vat, bottle filler, and case-conveyer which moves the cases from the bottle washer to the bottler.

The Reiss Dairy has in the past few years become one of the largest, best known and most trusted dairies in this section. Four trucks of the company give daily service to Sikeston, Matthews, New Madrid, Lilbourn, Marston, Canalou, Portageville, Hayti, Morehouse, Miner Switch, Bertrand, Charleston, Morley, Benton, Chaffee, Oran, Vanduser, Crowder, McMullin and intervening points. A program of expansion for the coming months is being worked out.

Mr. Reiss and his son-in-law, L. M. Standley, operate the business. Employees of the company are David Keasler, bob Lane, Henry Lane, Herschel Tyer, H. N. Bush, Ray Lee, J. L. Taylor, James Davenport, Murl Greenley, Raymond Agee, Marvin Wallace, and Leo Comstock.

"The Sikeston Herald" March 16, 1939
Pasteurized Milk – 5 Cents Per Pound

REISS DAIRY

No, there is no catch to the proposition. We have been selling milk for 5 cents per pound for several years. A quart of milk is equal to about 2.1 pounds and a quart of Reiss diary milk costs only 10 cents.

Milk compares very favorably with steak, eggs, bacon, and other foods in food value per pound of weight. Yet milk costs only 5 cents per pound. Considering the real food value, milk is less expensive than almost any food on the market. When you buy a quart of milk, you get MORE than your dime's worth.

It isn't necessary to advertise milk as a good source of vitamins. Milk contains all vitamins, and it is rated an excellent source of all vitamins except Vitamin C. Yet, you often see highly processed foods advertised as containing Vitamin A or D. Nature's nearest perfect food contains these vitamins in sufficient quantities to meet the body's needs. They do not have to be added artificially. Milk is truly the nearest perfect and the least expensive FOOD on the market today.

"The Sikeston Herald" March 30, 1939
"The Reiss Dairy Is Enlarging Building"

Work was started last Friday on an addition to the Reiss Dairy building here. The new addition will increase the width of the building 15 feet and will be added on the west side. The length of the new addition will be 70 feet.

The new addition, being built to take care of the present crowded condition and preparation for equipment later on, is being constructed of tile and glass.

The interior of the building will be of glazed tile for 3.5 feet above the floor and then four feet of glass will be added on top of the glazed tile. Above the glass additional tile will be added but this will have a somewhat different appearance and purpose than the lower glazed tile.

The glazed tile inside will aid in preventing the formation of as much moisture as forms inside the present building. The outside walls will be of glass brick, a composition which is made of 6-inch blocks and is four inches thick. This glass brick will aid in keeping out the heat in the hot weather and keeping the heat in during the winter months. The glass used inside for partitions will be plain glass so that visibility will be insured.

The present building will not be torn away, according to the management, but the new outside walls will cause the building to appear completely new. Later the present building may be done over inside to match the interior of the new addition.

John Setterfield is contractor in charge of the work and materials are being secured from the local lumber companies. It is expected that work will be completed on the new addition in about a month.

"The Sikeston Herald" May 18, 1939

NOTICE OF ADOPTION OF TRADE NAME

The undersigned has adopted for use a name, mark or device to identify and make known the ownership of cans, bottles and other vessels, owned and used by the undersigned in the manufacture, sale and distribution of milk, buttermilk and ice cream, and has had said name, mark or device printed, stamped, engraved, etched, blown, painted, or otherwise permanently fixed upon said cans, bottles and other vessels.

A description of said name, mark or device is as follows:

SIKESTON MISSOURI — Reiss DAIRY — PASTEURIZED PRODUCTS

The above notice is published herewith in three consecutive issues of The Sikeston Herald, a newspaper printed and published in the county and State in which is located the main office and headquarters of the undersigned Reiss Dairy, in accordance with the provisions of Section 12449, R. S. Mo., 1929.

> REISS DAIRY.
> By J. J. Reiss and
> L. M. Standley,
> Owners.

"The Sikeston Herald" February 8, 1940
"Modernization at Reiss Dairy Plant"

The largest and most modern dairy plant in this section of the State is the Reiss Dairy located at 523 East Malone Avenue in an attractive, well-equipped building which this year was enlarged to its present size of 48 by 72 feet.

The addition to the building erected this year, and which is 18 by 72 feet in size, is of buff colored tile with glass-brick window openings. Present plans are to replace the old portion of the building with tile as soon as possible.

Glass-brick was used, not only because it gives an attractive appearance but because it prevents dust and soot from entering the plant through the windows. Tile is being used in the building, which is fast being practically rebuilt, for its appearance, durability, and the quality of preventing rapid temperature changes to the contents of the building.

The interior of the building is divided into several rooms or compartments for the various operations necessary in the care of them and to systemize the work.

Across the front of the building are the stock and supply room, the sales room, and the office, which are white-enameled and lighted with fluorescent lights. To the rear is the pasteurizing room with the adjoining refrigerated storage room.

The pasteurizing room, with a floor space of about 450 square feet, contains most of the machinery necessary to process the milk, including a pump capable of pumping 12,000 pounds of milk per hour, a combined clarifier and separator costing $2,400; four spray pasteurizers each holding 150 gallons; a small pasteurizer with a capacity of 50 gallons for pasteurizing sweet cream; two surface coolers, one with a capacity of 3,000 pounds per hour, used for cooling sweet milk, and another with a capacity of 500 pounds per hour used for cooling skim milk and sweet cream. A bottling machine capable of filling and capping 55 bottles per minute is also part of the equipment of this room.

The refrigerated storage room is about 10 by 22 feet and is automatically cooled by refrigerated brine which in turn has been chilled by a York refrigerating unit. The by-products room is near the center of the building and is used for churning butter and making cottage cheese as well as packing these products. The receiving room and laboratory are on the west side of the building where all milk and cream are received.

In the receiving room are the weigh tank scales, and receiving vat with an automatic can washer. In the laboratory are Babcock Tester for butterfat and several other tests used regularly in the dairy business. Rolling conveyors bring in the full cans and take out the empty ones. In the rear are three more rooms – one for the storage of empty bottles and cases and an automatic bottle washer, a boiler room, a boiler room and the locker and washroom which is equipped with a shower bath for use of the employees.

The plant is compact and as much manual labor as possible is eliminated. All cases and bottles travel on conveyors and all milk is piped from one piece of equipment to another. All equipment coming in contact with the milk is stainless steel and is disassembled, washed, and sterilized at least once a day.

The inside walls and ceilings are of cement plaster enameled white, except the wainscoting, which is buff colored tile. All partitions have glass above the wainscoting which permits light to reach all parts of the building and also allows one to see from one end of the plant to the other. The floors are of concrete sloped in such a manner as to be self-draining. The lighting where needed most is fluorescent. All electric wires are in conduit and are protected in that way from moisture.

The Reiss Dairy operates four routes: one route extends as far south as Hayti, and includes Morehouse; another goes as far north as Benton and Chaffee; the third route is the wholesale route for Sikeston and Charleston and the fourth is almost exclusively retail deliveries in Sikeston. Another truck is operated about half time and the sixth truck is a relief vehicle used only when some other truck is undergoing repairs. Special and phone orders are delivered by bicycle.

At present time thirteen men are employed full time by Reiss Dairy, so on trucks and the others in the plant. The total payroll for 1939 exceeded $13,000, a sizeable sum for a plant of its size. "All employees must have health certificate before being permitted to work.

To the dairymen of the Sikeston vicinity, Reiss Dairy paid over $80,000 during 1939 for diary products. Farmers and dairymen realized a percentage of the gross sales in excess of the average of dairies throughout the U. S.

Reiss Dairy purchased three new delivery trucks during 1939 to add to its equipment. No new routes were established.

Other equipment purchased ruing the year included the following: a DeLaval Separator and Clarifier, Waukesha Milk Pump, complete receiving room equipment, an insulated stainless steel pasteurizer, one recording thermometer, almost 400 new milk crates, and over $4,000 work of milk bottles. This added equipment helped make Reiss Dairy the best equipped dairy in this section of Missouri.

Among the customers, the U. S. Government was one of the best, milk being supplied to three CCC Camps for the entire year and a fourth camp for the latter part of the year. At the present time, milk is being sold to the CCC Camps at New Madrid, Hayti, Popular Bluff, and Doniphan. The plant is inspected regularly by the U. S. Veterinary Inspector and has not failed of approval since its first inspection in July 1935. At present the dairy has 28 approved procedures who supply its entire output of milk.

In 1940, the Reiss Dairy hopes to install more equipment to further raise the quality of its products. On the proposed list of improvements and additions are the following: a homogenizer, larger refrigerated storage space, Vitamin D Milk and most of all: better service and higher quality of products.

At the present time a relatively full line of dairy products is being handled, but other products may be added before the year is far gone. Among the products now handled besides pasteurized sweet milk are cultured buttermilk, coffee and whipping cream, cottage cheese, butter, Bireley's Orangeade, and chocolate milk.

The firm is owned by John J. Reiss and L. M. Standley. Mr. Reiss' duties include the supervision of all producers and Mr. Standley is more concerned with the plant and office management. The Reiss Dairy invites you to visit and inspect its plant at any time.

"The Sikeston Herald" May 23, 1940
"Reiss Dairy has enlarged program"

J. J. Reiss and L. M. Standley, owners and managers of the Reiss Dairy, this week are extending a special invitation to Sikestonians to visit and inspect their newly-enlarged plant at 523 East Malone Avenue. An employee will conduct visitors through the plant, explaining the various processes.

Several extensive changes have been made, including an enlarged engine room for the boiler, refrigeration machinery, coal bin, garage space for two trucks, increased cold storage space to one-third more space, and the by-products room – churning, cottage cheese making, etc. – has been doubled in size. Space for empty bottles and cases has also been doubled so that all milk bottles and cases may now be stacked inside the plant.

A new York air-conditioning unit was purchased so that the temperature in the cold storage room would stay at 40 degrees all the time. The present York refrigeration plant was completely overhauled at the cost of several hundred dollars.

All loading and unloading is to be done by using case conveyors so that much unnecessary labor may be eliminated. Cases of milk are loaded directly from the cold storage room to the delivery trucks.

The new outside walls are of buff colored brick and tile and have four large glass brick windows. Ventilating is done with small casement sash near the top of each window. All outside openings are screen to keep our flies.

New machinery to be installed in the next few days includes a 300-gallon per our homogenizer and materials for supplying Vitamin D milk. Homogenized Vitamin D milk is a special milk for small children or other people who cannot digest the regular grades of milk. This bottled milk will be protected by a cover-cap.

"The Sikeston Herald" June 20, 1940
"Foolish Talk"

People are prone to engage in useless and foolish talk under stress and during times of unusual events. And also, during such conditions and times verbal expressions of people are often misunderstood.

During these days of stress and unusual events, caused by the terrible war in Europe, we are all prone to express our views too emphatically and we are also prone to exaggerate the views of other people who do not agree with our views. And, of course, it is quite easy to quote other people incorrectly.

Such has been the case during the past week in regard to some comment made by our good friend and splendid townsman, John J. Reiss, who has been represented as saying things complimentary to the present chancellor of Germany.

Nothing could be farther from the truth. Mr. Reiss is, it is true, a descendant of German parentage. So are thousands of other good and loyal American citizens. His ancestors left Germany many years ago because they wanted to live in such a land as America offered more than

TO THE PUBLIC:

We, the following employees of Reiss Dairy, Sikeston, Mo., wish to state that at no time have we heard Mr. J. J. Reiss make an unpatriotic statement, or any statement in support of Hitler at any time. Also, that there has been nobody discharged from this plant within the last year.

We will appreciate a continuance of your patronage.

This statement is made by the employees of the Reiss Dairy at our own free will, and without the advice or suggestion of any person or persons.

BOB LANE	PAUL D. ALLEN
HARVEY BUSH	IRA FENNIMORE
J. L. TAYLOR	WILLIAM WOOD
CHAS. TANNER	RAY DAVIS
EDDIE SHELBY	CECIL DAVIS
CLEM HOOVER	LYNN SUTTON
RAY LEE	GEO. F. BARTLETT
JOHN R. COWELL	MURELL GREENLEE

MARVIN WALLACE (Buddy)
JOHN HERSCHEL TYER

they wanted to live in their ancestral home. They made some sacrifices to come to America, but they knew they would gain more by coming. And they did.

Mr. Reiss has, by hard work and intelligent planning, become one of Sikeston's leading citizens, farmers and businessmen. He has an ardent love for the land which has given him the opportunity to succeed. He owes no allegiance to any other land than this and he would sacrifice, if necessary, everything he has to defend and protect this nation.

The question John Reiss' patriotism is to reflect on one's own loyalty. To accuse him of expressing sympathy for any dictatorship of Europe is to voice a charge that is not true and will not be given even a passing thought by anyone who knows John Reiss and his worth to this good community.

On page four of this issue are statements from the employees of Mr. Reiss and also from community leaders expressing their confidence in Mr. Reiss and his loyalty and worth as a citizen. These statements, of themselves, should be sufficient proof that any reports to the contrary are the products of malicious or thoughtless people.

"The Sikeston Herald" June 20, 1940
"Reiss Adds New Milk Processing Machine"

"You can't make butter out of milk that has passed through a homogenizer," said John J. Reiss, founder of the Reiss Dairy, this week, "but such milk is more easily digested and for that reason is better than other milk for infants and children, for sick people, and for the aged."

The Reiss Dairy is installing a homogenizer in the dairy plant here this week and expects to have it in operation within the next week or ten days.

The homogenizer is a machine which changes the physical structure of milk by breaking up the fat globules and casein and making the entire milk mass of the same structure throughout. This is done by subjecting the fluid to a pressure of 2500 pounds per square inch. Nothing is either added to or taken from the milk and its food properties remain the same. The only effect on the fluid is to make it more easily digested.

"The adding of the homogenizer is in line with our general policy of giving our patrons the best in milk products that is possible and keeping abreast of the times in the better processing of milk. No increase in price is planned for our homogenized milk," said Mr. Reiss.

"The Sikeston Herald" June 27, 1940
Public Notice

To the Public and Many Friends:

A friend in need is a friend indeed. Words fail me in expressing my deep appreciation of the help my friends have been to me in suppressing the false talk that has been circulated in the last few weeks about my loyalty to my country.

I prize my American citizenship very highly, and anyone who charges me with anything different does it with malice toward me.

JOHN J. REISS

"The Sikeston Herald" August 29, 1940
"Five Years of Steady Growth for Sikeston Industry"

Picture of Reiss Dairy Plant Today

Five years ago, the Reiss Dairy plant was moved from the J. J. Reiss farm east of Sikeston to its present location immediately west of the International Shoe Co. factory on Highway 60.

Its structural growth as depicted in the above picture has been surpassed only by the quality of products now offered by the plant and purchased all over Southeast Missouri by a long list of customers. Equipment, employees and production has shown a steady increase from year to year. Today the plant is one of the most progressive and modern of Sikeston industries. In its expansion, the Reiss Dairy has met the rapid growth of Sikeston particularly, well keeping pace with the city.

Our Fifth Anniversary

Only five short years since we moved our entire plant equipment from the farm to the small frame structure shown in top picture above.

The equipment included one 100-gallon pasteurizer, a small milk cooler, a hand bottler, small cream separator, a cottage cheese vat, a 51 H. P. boiler and miscellaneous smaller equipment. We had only four employees at that time, and only one delivery truck, (the picture was made several months after we moved in our "new home" and shows two Reiss Dairy trucks, one milk-producer's truck and five employees).

Our present equipment includes five stainless steel lined pasteurizers (four 150-gallon and one 50-gallon); a homogenizer, a combined DeLaval Airtight Separator and Clarifier with positive milk pump, a closed 2700-lb. per hour milk cooler, a thirty quart per minute automatic bottler, several hundred feet of stainless steel pipe and fittings, and recording thermometers for each pasteurizer all in the pasteurizing room.

Milk receiving room and laboratory room equipment includes a can washer, receiving tanks, scales, conveyors and equipment for various tests on milk and cream. Other equipment includes a stainless steel cottage cheese vat, a 400-pound churn, a Butter Printing Machine, an automatic bottle washer, a 25 H. P. boiler and a five-ton Refrigerating Machine with accessories. Other smaller units include cases and bottles, cans, etc. At present we operate six trucks—four full time and two part time, with a total of fourteen employees on trucks and in the plant.

Reiss Dairy and the employees wish to thank our Customers for making these improvements possible. By your continued support you have helped develop the best equipped Dairy in this section of Missouri. We have made improvements in the quality of our products and have added new products as the need justified—the latest of which were our Homogenized Milk and the Homogenized-Vitamin D Milk. It is our policy to adopt every possible improvement—both in method and machine—wherever possible. We invite your continued patronage.

SIKESTON MISSOURI *Reiss* DAIRY PASTEURIZED PRODUCTS

"The Sikeston Herald" February 13, 1941
"Expansion for the Reiss Dairy"

Reiss Dairy, located at 523 E. Malone, enjoyed another good year during 1940 with a total gain in business of approximately 26%. This increase was due largely to the increase of population in the territory served, the two CCC camps at Jackson and Delta, and the Missouri Institute of Aeronautics located at Sikeston.

At present the Reiss Dairy is operating four full time trucks and two part time. One route embraces the residential section of Sikeston and a few of the outlying stores and cafes; Bob Lane has operated this route for several years. The second route includes all grocery stores and cafes in Sikeston, the Missouri Institute of Aeronautics, Bertrand and Charleston, with Lynn Sutton in charge. The third route extends as far north as Jackson, including Oran, Chaffee, Benton, Delta, Illmo, Fornfelt, Morley, Vanduser, and intermediate stops, as well as CCC camps at Delta and Jackson. George Bartlett operates this route. The fourth or south route is operated by Herschel Tyer and extends to Hayti on the south with stops at Matthews, New Madrid, Lilbourn, Marston and Portageville. The route also includes Morehouse on the west and CCC scamps at New Madrid and Hayti.

New Additions and New Products – During 1940 Reiss Dairy spent over $5,000 on its present building in Sikeston to enable it to handle more efficiently its products. An addition of approximately 800 square feet was attached to the rear and east side of the building, the same being of brick and tile with self-supporting roof. Glass block windows are standard throughout the entire building, for they admit light and keep out dust and soot. The refrigerated storage room was enlarged one-third and other minor changes made in moving partitions, resurfacing floors, etc. In the plant several new pieces of equipment were bought. Included in the new equipment was a new 800-lb. churn, a 300-gallon per homogenizer, a butter printing machine, new refrigerating equipment and several hundred bottle crates. A total of $6,600 was spent for bottles, many of which have been lost or broken.

New products produced in 1940 include the homogenized grade "A" milk, vitamin "D" homogenized milk, egg nog mix, and ice cream mix. These products are in addition to the products previously processed. Probably the most popular new product ever processed by Reiss Dairy is the new homogenized milk. Approximately one in three customers drinks it and among cafes it is the unanimous choice. Ice cream mix was supplied to counter-freezer operators in Portageville, Morehouse, Sikeston, Chaffee, and Cape Girardeau. The egg nog mix was sold during the Christmas holidays, and – to prove it was popular – over 250 gallons were consumed.

Plans for 1941 – This year, Reiss Dairy plans to launch its improvement program. The building will not be enlarged but use will be made of waste space and consolidation of machinery space. The refrigerated storage room will be enlarged and a new milk-processing room will be built. New equipment will include an automatic bottle washer, replacing the present small one, new conveyors, and general rearrangement of machinery will be perfected. In keeping with its traditional policy of supplying the best possible products at reasonable costs, other improvements will be made with no expected increase in prices.

Market for Farmers – Reiss Dairy feels that it has had a part in creating a market for farm products. During 1940 it purchased over $100,000 worth of farm dairy products, two-thirds of which was milk and the rest was cream. The milk was produced on about twenty-five dairy farms approved by the U.S. CCC veterinarian – farms located in the territory from Oran to Kewanee and Bertrand to Gray Ridge.

Farmers in most instances received prices equal to or above those paid in the St. Louis or Memphis areas. Reiss Dairy paid to an average of 14 employees the sum of approximately $18,000. To the Board of Public Works it paid over $1600 for light, water and power. To prove that the newspapers and advertisers got their bit – about $1500 was spent for advertising.

Reiss Dairy is proud of its record. It is even more proud to be able to list several hundred families in Sikeston and surrounding country and towns as its regular patrons – many of whom have been users of Reiss Dairy products for several years. It is glad to be able to provide pure, safe wholesome dairy products to people in this section of Missouri, to such an extent that no cities in the territory served have felt that a milk ordinance was necessary to protect the health of its citizens. Such is the record that Reiss Dairy hopes to excel in 1941.

"The Sikeston Herald" March 20, 1941
Advertisement

Another Reiss Dairy Accomplishment

For several months Reiss Dairy has tried to get all approved milk-producing farms to install electrically operated milk coolers so that the milk coming to our plant during the summer months would still mee t our exacting requirements. It has been a task. Our producers have had to be informed how they could get more for their milk and at the same time sell more milk. They have been told that o e can of rejected milk would pay a month's expense of operation for the box. They have considered these factors—and this week twenty-three of our twenty-five approved farms have completed installation of milk coolers for the farms. One other will install his cooler in July when electric current is distributed near his farm. The other one may come in later.

Since the average cost of these boxes is about $300, you can see this is quite an investment. Last year Reiss Dairy purchased over $60,000 worth of fluid milk from these same producers, so they are now cooperating with us by helping improve the product we sell. They know that to remain on the approved list of Reiss Dairy producers, they must be making improvements in methods and equipment all the time. We have no way of knowing, but we are almost sure there is no Dairy in Southeast Miissouri with so large a per cent of its producers who have electrically operated farm milk coolers.

Reiss Dairy is constantly making improvements. We expect the same of our producers. They must be improving their methods and equipment to meet the ever-increasing restrictions of our health departments.

These producers will be glad to have you visit their farms and see how Reiss Dairy Grade "A" Milk is produced.

"The Sikeston Herald" June 12, 1941
"Recognition to Reiss Dairy by Magazine"

In the June issue of *Milk Plant Monthly*, trade magazine for dairy plants, the Reiss Dairy plant was given considerable publicity. The front page of the magazine used as its illustration the front view of the Reiss Dairy plant and employees. Elsewhere in the issue were five pages of reading matter and pictures about the plant.

The magazine headed the main article, "Continuous Program of Modernization and Clever Advertising of High-Quality Products Have Made Reiss Dairy of Sikeston, Missouri, a Progressive Profitable Business." The article was written by Howard Barman, feature writer for the magazine.

The article pointed out that modernization and enlargement was a part of the annual program of Reiss Dairy. It also pointed out that the owners, J. J. Reiss and L. M. Standley, attributed a large part of their program to the clever newspaper advertising program they maintained locally and throughout Southeast Missouri. The Reiss Dairy plant is six years old.

"The Sikeston Herald" August 28, 1941
Reiss Dairy Six Years Old
Rapid Expansion shown in Progressive Local Institution

The sixth anniversary of its establishment in Sikeston finds the Reiss Dairy, one of the town's leading business houses, with a prestige and reputation that is the envy of many longer-established businesses.

In August 1935, when the machinery was moved to town from John J. Reiss' farm a mile east of town to a small frame building on the site of the present structure, the dairy served only a small area in and around Sikeston/

Since that time, it has grown so that four full-time trucks and two part-time trucks are needed to make deliveries in Sikeston, Bertrand, Charleston, Oran, Chaffee, Benton, Delta, Illmo, Fornfelt, Morley, Vanduser, Matthews, New Madrid, Lilbourn, Marston, Portageville and Morehouse.

The Missouri Institute of Aeronautics and CCC camps at Hyati, Delta, New Madrid, and Jackson are also supplied with Reiss Dairy products.

During 1940, the annual records showed, the business of the Reiss Dairy increased more than 26 per cent, mainly because of the increase of population in the territory served and the opening of the air school here.

The most modern and efficient of dairy equipment is constantly being installed at the Reiss Dairy plant as the establishment strives to improve its products. All processes through which the milk and other products pass are mechanical and sanitary.

Mr. Reiss is assisted in the management of the dairy by his son-in-law L. M. Standley, to whom much of the credit for the rapid and solid growth of the establishment is due.

Since the first of the year, Mr. Standley reports, more than $7000 has been spent for new equipment remodeling of the plant and other work designed to provide safer, and more delicious and sanitary dairy products for Reiss Dairy customers.

The interior of the plant was rearranged to allow space for a separate bottling room, the storage room was increased, a bottle washer with twice the capacity of the old installed, and numerous other improvements made. Also, newly-installed is a plate-type heater and cooler, and within the near future, it is planned, a "short-time continuous" system will be installed. Two new trucks have also been added to the fleet of Reiss trucks recently.

In keeping with its traditional policy of supplying the best possible products at reasonable costs, other improvements will be made with no expected increase in prices.

Employees of the Reiss Dairy at present are H. M. Bush, Ray Lee Davis, Muri Greenlee, Cecil Davis, Eddie Shelby, Virlin Spivey, Leo Hinton, Albert Blizzell, Virgil Vaughn, Ruppert Lane, James Evans, Lynn Sutton, George Bartlett, J. H. Tyer Jr., Dick Taff, and Ruth Buchholz.

SIKESTON (MO.) HERALD   THURSDAY, AUGUST 28, 1941

6 Years of Rapid Growth
PROGRESSIVE RECORD OF
The REISS DAIRY

THE MODERN REISS DAIRY PLANT AS IT APPEARS TODAY

PICTURE OF REISS DAIRY PLANT SIX YEARS AGO

*I*n August, 1935, Reiss Dairy went to town from the Reiss Dairy farm. Six years have passed, and we are proud to say, Reiss Dairy has experienced steady and substantial growth and expansion. This growth can be attributed to a number of factors, among which are:

1 Improvement of quality by purchase of new and larger machinery—discarding the old and obsolete.

2 Maintaining fair prices for the products we buy and sell.

3 An ever-increasing confidence in the quality of Reiss Dairy products as shown by its increased use.

4 An increase in the variety of Reiss Dairy products sold.

5 Deliveries were speeded up. This enabled us to make many more deliveries per day.

6 Expansion of territory as well as an increase in population in the area Reiss Dairy serves.

Some Pertinent Facts about the Growth of Reiss Dairy—

		1935	1941
1.	Employees	3	17
2.	Producing Farms	2	23
3.	Bottling Capacity	90 Gal. Per Hour	450 Gallons Per Hour
4.	Refrigerating Storage Space	1200 Cubic Feet	3960 Cubic Feet
5.	Trucks	1	6
6.	Boiler Capacity	5 Horsepower	25 Horsepower
7.	Floor Space	1360 Square Feet	4224 Square Feet

Reiss Dairy also serves besides Sikeston territory as far north as Jackson, east as Wyatt, south as Hayti, and west as Essex. In addition four CCC Camps—Hayti, New Madrid, Delta and Jackson and the Missouri Institute of Aeronautics at Sikeston are served. Reiss Dairy and its producing farms are inspected regularly by U. S. CCC Veterinarian and its milk is classified Grade "A"

SIKESTON MISSOURI *Reiss* DAIRY   PASTEURIZED PRODUCTS

"The Sikeston Herald" September 4, 1941
Local Dairies Have "Milk Bottle Trouble"

Because of the shortage of milk bottles, some Sikeston dairies this week began the practice of charging a 1-cent deposit on the container. The charge will be added to the monthly milk bill if a bottle is not left by regular customers to take the place of the one being delivered by the milkman.

L. M. Standley, manager of Reiss Dairy, received a telegram yesterday morning stating that a quantity of bottles, ordered more than three months ago was being shipped and this supply it is hoped will ease the shortage for a time. Similar delay in receiving shipment has been experienced by other dairies.

The shortage of bottles became drastic Tuesday, when, because of stores being closed for the holiday, housewives did not return the bottles bought the previous day. Deliveries were several hours behind as the dairies rushed out the filled bottles almost as fast as the "empties" were returned.

"The Sikeston Herald" July 2, 1942
State Magazine Commends REA

Sikeston got some good publicity this week when the *Missouri Ruralist*, a bi-monthly trade journal of Missouri farmers, published a story telling how a local dairy-man, J. J. Reiss, and the local REA co-operatives, the Scott-New Madrid-Mississippi Co-operative Association, had cooperated in bringing about a better system of farming as well as insuring a more dependable and high grade milk supply for the district.

Successful Dairying – Electricity on the farm may mean more than just a convenience at the touch of a button or switch. It sometimes means a new system of farming, based on better and more uniform incomes.

Such a case is demonstrated by a growing milk and dairying industry development near Sikeston in southeast Missouri. Here in the land of cotton, dairying has been pretty much neglected.

However, Sikeston is enjoying a regular defense boom. A government school for training airplane pilots, plus a factory or so and a general thriving town have created a good milk market.

A large portion of the milk supply of the town is handled by J. J. Reiss who has a new and modern dairy plant. To enable his producers to give him a better quality milk, he has financed for his producers the purchase of electric milk coolers.

With the money which Mr. Reiss provided, 19 coolers have been installed. Two other farms have coolers so that 21 coolers are in operation, among the 23 producers that send milk to the Reiss Dairy.

Many of these producers are new at the business. Maybe the electricity was not the only factor that made their dairying possible – but without it few of them could compete in the business of getting fresh milk to town. Of the producers, 17 are on an REA line which has headquarters in Sikeston.

Mr. Reiss is more than pleased with the results of his program. He is getting much higher quality milk. "The plan has been more than satisfactory," he reported. Mr. Reiss is being repaid for the coolers at so much a week taken from the weekly milk checks. The average rate is $5 a week.

In return for buying the coolers, the producers owning them get a larger base allowed them, so that they really get to sell more milk at the top process than those without coolers.

"It took a lot of effort on my part to talk my producers into buying the coolers," Mr. Reiss admits, "but now they are glad to have them." The coolers, which we bought in one group, are of the 3- and 4-can type. A banquet for the new owners of the coolers was another goodwill gesture by Mr. Reiss. Here is where rural electricity has really meant something to is users.

"The Sikeston Herald" January 11, 1945
Joint advertisement by Reiss Dairy and Woods Dairy

"The Sikeston Herald" August 30, 1945

Your Best Source of Dairy Products

1935   1945

SINCE 1935

Since 1935, Reiss Dairy has been your best source of safe, wholesome dairy products. From a very small beginning, Reiss Dairy has always tried to give the best service possible under existing conditions. Growth and expansion have been gradual as more and more people called for more and more Reiss Dairy Milk, making this growth possible.

Some Advantages to You of Using Regularly Reiss Dairy Products Are:

1. Safe, Wholesome Dairy Products.

2. Reasonable prices for superior products.

3. Prompt and regular delivery service.

4. The only Dairy Homogenizing Milk in the Sikeston area.

5. The only Dairy Churning Butter in the Sikeston area.

6. The only Dairy making Cottage Cheese in the Sikeston area.

7. The only plant in the Sikeston area that has all milk handling equipment constructed of Stainless Steel.

8. The only plant located in the city—ready to serve you at any time.

9. Our guarantee of satisfaction or your money refunded.

Come visit us any time—we may be pretty busy, but we can stop long enough to show you around.

1935 - 1945   SIKESTON MISSOURI  PASTEURIZED PRODUCTS   1935 - 1945

"The Daily Standard, September 22, 1947
Services Today at Baptist Church for Mrs. Reiss

Mrs. John J. Reiss, aged 63 years, died at her home 721 Sikes Avenue, early Saturday morning after a prolonged illness of carcinoma.

Funeral services were conducted at the Sikeston Baptist Church by her pastor, the Rev. E. D. Owen, at 2:30 o'clock this afternoon and interment was in Memorial Park Cemetery with Welsh service.

Mrs. Reiss, as Etta Sellards, the daughter of Mr. and Mrs. A. Sellards, was born near Fredericktown, in Madison County, November 11, 1884.

On January 24, 1910, Miss Sellards became the wife of John J. Reiss. After living for a time at Flat River and later near Matthews, Mr. and Mrs. Reiss came to Sikeston in 1910, buying a farm east of Sikeston, where Mr. Reiss established the Reiss Farm Dairy, planted the Reiss Peach Orchard and they became leaders in church, civic and agricultural circles.

Two years ago they sold their farm and moved to the present residence on Sikes Avenue. Mrs. Reiss had been a member of the Baptist Church since childhood and had always taken a lively interest in its activities.

Surviving are her husband and two daughters, Miss Audrey Reiss, now employed by the Scott County Farm equipment Company, and Mrs. L. M. Standley, whose husband is associated with her father in the Reiss Diary; two grandchildren, Jo Ellen and Kay Standley. Also surviving are a brother, John Sellards of Route 2, Sikeston, and a sister, Mrs. Milburn Arbaugh of Sikeston.

"The Daily Standard" October 1, 1947

Plans Announced for New Reiss Dairy Plant on 61 South

Plans for anew dairy plant to be located on Highway 61 a half block south of Gladys Street have been announced by the Reiss Dairy. The new plant which will contain 12,000 square feet of floor space, will house the plant, office, cold storage, and a dairy bar.

Of brick construction on the outside, the plant will have tile and glass construction on the inside. There are 3 acres of ground which will provide plenty of parking space so as ot to interfere with the operation of the plant.

A new plant for the Reiss Dairy has been a dream of the owners, John J. Reiss and son-in-law, L. M. Standley, for several years. Pictured is a scale model of the proposed new plant as prepared by R. Paul Buckmueller, architect. The model is now on display in a window at the J. C. Penny Store.

In early 1946 planes began to be made for its construction. Sheets of paper by the dozens were used for suggested plant layouts. Trade publications, services of the state university, machinery manufacturers and jobbers, and others were called on to help crystalize these plans.

The final plan is not the work of the architect or any single individual. It represents ideas from dozens of sources. The milk flow plan is the simplest possible – a straight line – which eliminated costly operations of the processing plant.

Plans so far have been approved by the Missouri State Division of Health. Final approval is withheld until complete plans are examined. Sanitation and ease of cleaning are given primary consideration in planning the building. All material used in the plant will be fireproof and must be of a material that can be washed regularly.

An innovation not usually found in dairy plants is the Milk Bar where a complete line of dairy products are offered for sale, to be consumed at the Dairy Bar or taken home for use there. The Dairy Bar will have a seating accommodation for about 60 persons and parking space for at least 100 cars.

The Reiss Dairy has been in operation approximately 21 years, having been started on a farm east of Sikeston about 1926. It was the first dairy in the Sikeston area to pasteurize milk. Pasteurizing was begun about 1930. The first customer of the Reiss Farm Dairy was the Sellard's Meat a Market. Two dairy plant buildings were erected on the farm, the first of which burned.

In 1935 the first plant was built in Sikeston by adding to and remodeling a restaurant building. This building has been improved and enlarged three or four times and the original building has been more than doubled in size. The present plant building will be retained, mostly for storage space.

The business was founded on bottled whole milk, which to this day is the chief product sold. Churning of surplus cream into butter was probably the second product manufactured. Chocolate milk, buttermilk, cottage cheese followed in about that order. The Reiss Dairy was the first dairy in southern Missouri to bottle homogenized milk, a service which was started about 1940. Ab out 70 per cent of all bottled milk sold is homogenized at present.

Manufacture of ice cream mix has become a definite part of processing operations since 1940, most of which is sold to counter-freezers in and near Sikeston. The manufacture and sale of ice cream is provided for in the new building.

Hand filling of bottles was replaced with a small filling machine in 1933. This original machine has been replaced twice, until now milk is bottled at the rate of 5000 pounds per hour.

Hand washing of bottles was replaced by machine washing in 1936. The original machine has been replaced and now an eight-wide soaker washer with automatic infeed and unload enables one operator to wash 80 bottles per minute.

Vat or holding method is used for pasteurizing milk, but new equipment is in the plant ready to be installed in the new building. This equipment will speed up and simplify pasteurizing operations. New equipment on order include a 650-gallon per hour homogenizer, a 2000-gallon refrigerated storage tank, continuous ice cream freezer, new refrigeration machinery and milk receiving room equipment.

Reiss Dairy started business in Sikeston only. When CCC camps were established in New Madrid and Hayti, a route was started into that territory. Now towns served extend from Benton and Chaffee on the north to Caruthersville and Hayti on the south, Parma and Gray Ridge on the west to Bertrand and East Prairie on the east – an average radius of about 30 miles.

Because of the farming setup in Southeast Missouri, dairy cows and dairying have never been a large industry. Twenty years ago hardly a can of cream and no milk were produced for sale to dairies.

About 15 years ago Reiss Dairy purchased the first milk from the C. D. Brewer herd. Since that time dairy farmers have become interested in producing milk so that today about 150 farms are producing milk for Reiss Dairy. Approximately two thirds of this volume is of a quality that could be bottled as Grade A.

Constant supervision and encouragement by the Reiss Dairy ownership has enabled Reiss Dairy to improve the quality of milk received as well as increasing volume to meet ever increasing demands.

Although a quart of milk costs about twice as much as it did in Depression days, the farmers are receiving 230 per cent of the price paid in 1934-5 for quality milk. High feed and operating costs on the farm are a major factor in increasing the cost of milk to the consumer. A dairy cow that sold for $30 to $40 in 1935 now costs the dairyman a neat $200.

"The Sikeston Herald" February 19, 1948

"The Sikeston Herald" March 11, 1948

No Bottle Deposit . . . .

No deposit is now required on any Reiss
Dairy containers. Deposits are a nuisance—to
you, the grocer and to us.

Naturally we expect our customers to
return bottles because that is one reason we
can keep milk prices lower than any other city
in Southeast Missouri.

Your cooperation is much appreciated.

SIKESTON MISSOURI *Reiss* DAIRY PASTEURIZED PRODUCTS

"The Sikeston Herald" August 19, 1948
"Construction Progress at Reiss Dairy Plant"

The elaborate, ultra-modern one-story plant being erected for the Reiss Dairy, begun in early January, will be ready to be fully \occupied about Christmas, Lonnie M. Standley, manager, said today. The new dairy distributing plant is located on the east side of Highway 61 one-half block south of East Gladys Street.

The building is of cream-colored brick exterior with interior of white glazed tile. The tile is being installed at present, and the storage room is now under construction. A bulldozer is now in operation preparing the grounds for landscaping at the front of the building. The plant's dimensions are 100 by 100 feet.

A feature of the new dairy will be a milk bar and soda fountain. Upon occupying their new plant Reiss Dairy will begin making ice cream, which with sandwiches, chocolate milk, and orangeade, will be served to customers.

Reiss buys milk from 120 different milk producers. John J. Reiss, founder, began his dairy business in 1928 on his farm and moved to the present location at 523 East Malone Street in 1935. The diary sells butter, cottage cheese, chocolate milk whipping and coffee creams, in addition to the main milk line and also bottles and sells orangeade.

Reiss Dairy products are distributed mainly along Highway 61, both north and south of Sikeston. The most distant points south are Caruthersville and Hayti, and the extreme northern outlet is Chaffee. East Prairie to the southeast, and Gray Ridge to the west, are also served by Reiss Dairy trucks.

"The Daily Standard" January 25, 1949

Why – Reiss Dairy New Dairy Plant

The value of good dairy products cannot be estimated until you see how they are handled.

Reiss Dairy has spent thousands of dollars, in addition to the cost of the new building, to bring to you the best in dairy products. Nowhere in Missouri will you find a more modern dairy plant with more efficient plant equipment. It is a marvel, even to those accustomed to being around dairies, to see the machinery in operation that almost automatically brings to you milk that meets the dairy's own and your own high standards of quality, flavor and wholesomeness.

Hundreds of feet of spotless stainless steel pipe, tanks and equipment of sanitary stainless steel, machines that eliminate the human hand from even touching the milk, all these and many more features are yours in a bottle of Reiss Dairy milk.

And remember this—no health authority has ever asked or ordered Reiss Dairy to build a new building or install this equipment. It is Reiss Dairy's answer to your confidence in its dairy products.

Opening date to be announced soon.

Reiss DAIRY

Pasteurized Products

"The Sikeston Herald" February 3, 1949
"Formal Opening of Reiss Dairy Plant"

New, Modern Home of the Reiss Dairy

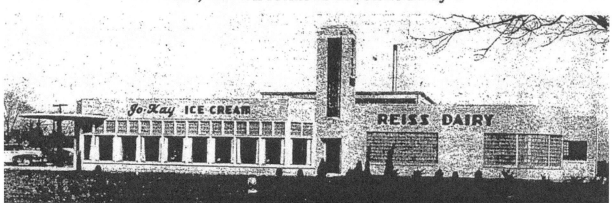

Beginning Saturday February 5 and continuing until next Tuesday evening will be the formal opening of the new Reiss Dairy processing plant and equipment.

The Cow Bell, a café specializing in dairy products foods, which is housed in the Reiss Dairy building and has already proven to be a popular place for those wanting light lunches and snacks, was formally opened January 1, with Mr. and Mrs. B. D. Blackburn as managers.

The new building and equipment of the Reiss Dairy is literally a dream come true. Its owners and managers have long wanted a building of such attractiveness as to be an ornament to the progressive community in which it is located and of such size as to house a business that had long since outgrown its former location.

After many months of inspecting other modern dairy processing plants and planning the new plant here, the new Reiss Dairy building was begun just a year ago on a three-acre tract of land on Highway 61 in the southeastern part of Sikeston.

The history of Reiss Dairy is one of progress. A few of the "firsts" that can be attributed to advances made by the firm in the dairy field are:

1. First dairy to process and sell pasteurized milk in the Sikeston area.
2. First dairy in Sikeston to make cottage cheese, butter, and chocolate milk.
3. First dairy in Sikeston to process and sell homogenized milk. In fact the first dairy in rural Missouri to homogenize milk.
4. First dairy in Sikeston to service outlying towns with dairy products.
5. First dairy in Sikeston to use all stainless steel equipment in processing dairy products.

Reiss Dairy has grown from a small beginning when back about 1928, John J. Reiss started delivering a few quarts of milk to stores and homes in Sikeston. At that time many people in Sikeston had their own cows or purchased their dairy needs from their neighbors. The first Reiss Dairy plant was a building on the farm about 12 feet square which was later destroyed by fire. It was replaced by one slightly larger. This one in turn was replaced by a still larger plant located on the farm. This building was about 18 feet by 30 feet and had a cold storage room built in it. It was in this building that Mr. Reiss installed his first pasteurizer about 1931. Business grew steadily, even during the depression years, and other dairy products were processed – butter, cottage cheese, chocolate milk and buttermilk.

In 1935, Mr. Reiss decided that a dairy plant in Sikeston would be an asset to his business and a convenience for the customers, so he purchased a restaurant building at 523 E. Malone Avenue. This building was remodeled and an addition made thereto so that there would be enough room for a dairy plant, cold storage room and office. In the years 1936-41 this building was enlarged several times to make room for a growing business. Larger and more efficient equipment was installed as time went on until Reiss Dairy became one of the largest producers in this area.

Trade territory was added until Reiss Dairy trucks gave daily delivery service to cities as far away as Caruthersville, East Prairie, and Chaffee. Six trucks are now used to deliver dairy products in Sikeston and other towns. Six routes are necessary to pick up milk from farms, much of this milk going back over the same roads used to haul the milk to the diary plant.

The new Reiss Dairy plant is a result of years of planning. New equipment was placed on order for the new plant as early as 1945. The size of the plant, the layout of the various rooms and departments was seriously studied for several months before the architect started work. Preliminary drawings of floor plans were made by the dozens, but finally after consultation with dairy engineers and the architect, R. Paul Buchmueller, a floor plan was made that met the enthusiastic response of the owners. It embraced two buildings with about 12,000 square feet of floor space, the larger building housing the dairy bar, offices and dairy plant, the smaller building being a heating plant building.

The diary plant building is designed so the two offices and the dairy bar occupy the entire front of the building with the dairy plant to the rear.

The central office is just to the right of the font entrance as you enter the building. A window has been installed for the convenience of the customers so that business may be transacted with a minimum of confusion. Desks and filing cabinets are conveniently arranged for office personnel and a lavatory and a cloakroom are included in the space allotted for the office. A smaller private office for the owners is located adjacent to the central office. The offices and "Cow Bell" are heated by a hot air circulating unit in winter and cooled by cold air in summer. Another feature of the office arrangement is a specially designed area where salesmen may check into the office and complete their reports.

In the center of the dairy building is a large processing and packaging room. This is an area some 2500 square feet. The walls are glazed tile, the ceiling aluminum enameled white and the floors are white concrete. Ample floor drains have been provided to care for surface water on the floor. All doors are steel enameled white. This room houses dozens of pieces of equipment both large and small necessary to the processing of dairy products. A large milk receiving room is located at the rear of the building on the south side. In this room milk is received from the farms, weighed, graded, and tested, the empty cans are washed and returned to the farms. A large machinery room is located in the rear in which is located refrigeration machinery so necessary in processing milk as well as power and lighting panel boards. Along the north side of the building are two insulated milk and ice cream storage rooms. Provision has been made so that dairy products can be easily loaded on trucks for delivery to stores and consumers. Adequate shower, locker and toilet facilities have been provided for plant personnel. The entire building is of fireproof material. The front of the building is cream-colored brick and rear faced with red brick. The roof is steel supported and is insulated with fire-proof material. A driveway entirely around the building is used by trucks delivering milk to the building and loading for delivery to the trade. A half acre parking lot on the north side of the building is for use of customers of the "Cow Bell."

Business institutions like Reiss Dairy and the modern plant just completed could not exist unless someone caused them to exist. In the case of the Reiss Dairy and its buildings and equipment, the people who caused them to exist for this week's inspection and for future service to a growing community were John J. Reiss and his son-in-law, Lonnie M. Standley, owners and managers of the dairy business which bears the name of the former and its founder.

Mr. Reiss is a native of Illinois, having been born near Belleville in that state in 1877. His diary experience also began in that city and he was later connected with dairies at Floraville, Ill., and Flat River, Mo. Other preparation for his successful business experience were courses of study in dairying at Illinois and Missouri State Universities.

In 1909 Mr. Reiss came to Southeast Missouri and for ten years he operated the W. H. Andrews farm near Matthews now owned by Mr. and Mrs. Oscar Carroll. In 1919 he bought a farm east of Sikeston, where he lived until six years ago, moving to Sikeston in 1942.

In 1910 Mr. Reiss married Miss Etta Sellards, who passed away in 1947. Their two daughters are Lillian (Mrs. L. M. Standley) of Sikeston and Miss Audrey Reiss of Phoenix, Ariz.

In addition to his busy life as a farmer and dairyman, Mr. Reiss has always had time to give to the civic and religious interests of his community. He has long been an official member of the First Baptist Church of Sikeston and has served as its Sunday School superintendent. He has served as president of the Scott County Farm Bureau, as chairman of the Scott County Red Cross and in many other helpful capacities.

Mr. Standley is a native of Southeast Missouri, having been born near Poplar Bluff in 1907. He attended Washington University in St. Louis and State College at Cape Girardeau, receiving his degree as Bachelor of Science at the latter school. For several years he taught school in St. Louis County, coming to Sikeston and joining Mr. Reiss in the dairy business in 1935.

In 1934 Mr. Standley was married to Miss Lillian Reiss and they have two daughters, Jo Ellen, 10 and Kay, 7. It is for the two girls that one of the products of the Reiss Dairy, "Jo-Kay Ice Cream" is named.

Mr. Standley, too, has taken a lively interest in community affairs of his home district. Being a member of the Methodist Church, he has served as chairman of the official board and as Sunday School superintendent of the Sikeston Church and at present is a member of the board of stewards. In 1938 he was president of the Kiwanis Club of Sikeston and is now one of the leaders in that service club. In 1944 he served as president of the Sikeston Chamber of Commerce. In Boy Scout work he has been a prominent leader, as he has in many other civic endeavors.

"The Sikeston Herald" April 20, 1950

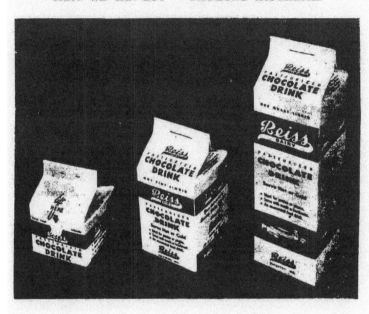

"The Sikeston Herald" – September 10, 1951
Important Persons at Reiss Dairy

These are the men who operate the Reiss Dairy Plant – you seldom see them – yet each one has an important part in the production of fine GRADE "A" REISS DAIRY PRODUCTS.
MARVIN "BUDDY" WALLACE Assistant Plant Foreman – Cottage Cheese and Jo-Kay Ice Cream maker. Owns his home on Helen Street, has four boys and a girl. Has worked at Reiss Dairy 13 years. A World War II veteran.

RAY LEE Plant Foreman – with 15 years experience at Reiss Dairy. Super vises entire plant operation. Owns his home on Virginia Street, has one son Jimmy who is attending State College at Cape.

ROBERT "BOB" ATKINSON Maintenance Engineer – Installs new equipment and maintains operating machinery. Lives on Greer Street, owns his home. Has a boy and a girl. A veteran of World War II. Has been with Reiss Dairy since 1945.

EMORY OLIVER Pasteurizing Man – Assembles and operates pasteurizing machinery. Lives in Airport addition. An employee of Reiss Dairy three years.

RAY VICK Pasteurizing Man – Assembles and operates pasteurizing machinery. Attends State College at Cape in winter.

CLYDE PAYLOR Maintenance – Owns home on Dorothy Street. An employee of Reiss Dairy since 1946.

LESLIE HUMES Pure-Pak Operator – Packages Reiss Dairy products. Owns his home on Murray Lane. Has four boys and a girl. Three years experience with Reiss Dairy.

HURSHEL BAILEY Ice Cream Mix Maker – Lives on east Hunter Street. Has three boys. A veteran of World War II. Six years experience at Reiss Dairy.

MERRILL HAYS Pure-Pak Operator – An employee since 1946. Has one daughter. Lives on Gladys Street.

HANSEL DUNCAN Cold Storage Man – Two years service at Reiss Dairy. Lives on Gladys Street. Has one boy.

LEONARD McGEE Maintenance – One year's experience at Reiss Dairy. Has two children. Lives on Ruth Street.

MURL GREENLEE Pure-Pak Operator – An employee of Reiss Dairy for eight years. Owns his home on Bynum Street. Has one girl and one boy.

HUGH GOODE Weigher and Tester – Missouri licensed buyer and tester for milk and cream. One year's experience at Reiss Dairy. Has four children.

WALTER McVEIGH Maintenance – Eight year's experience at Reiss Dairy. Owns home on Smith Avenue.

Reiss Dairy operates a profit-sharing plan for all plant and office personal with one or more years. This plan is in its fifth year of operation,

Above: Beside their new refrigerated Milk and Jo-Kay Ice Cream trucks are the friendly salesmen who deliver Reiss Dairy Grade "A" Dairy Products and Jo-Kay Ice Cream to your Food Store. On the left: Mr. Atlas Hatley, a Reiss Dairy salesman since 1948. Mr. and Mrs. Hatley own their own home in Sikeston—they have three children. At present Mr. Hatley is recovering from surgery at the Missouri Delta Hospital.
On the right: Mr. E. H. Spivey has been with Reiss Dairy since 1943—an employee for over twelve years. In all this time, Mr. Spivey has never had a truck accident. Mr. and Mrs. Spivey own their home on North Street.

"The Sikeston Herald" October 25, 1951

The Course of True Love
Seldom Runs Smooth . . .

Few people realize the problems involved in meeting the requirments of our customers as regards dairy products

For instance - - - a year ago, many of you were asking when Reiss Dairy would be Grade 'A'. In the short time of 10 months, Reiss Dairy is not merely making 'passing grades' (Grade A is 75%) but has become an 'E STUDENT' (Approved Dairy above 90%)

Three weeks ago, Reiss Dairy started production on a new Buttermilk

Country Style Buttermilk

the style of Buttermilk so familiar to so many of our customers. Mind you, this was an idea of a Reiss Dairy Salesman 'Doc' Shy.

Now 9 out of 10 bottles of Reiss Dairy Buttermilk sold are:

Country Style Buttermilk

"The Sikeston Herald" December 6, 1951
Local Dairy Announces Price Increase on Milk

Reiss Dairy announced this week a price increase in milk on home deliveries. Milk to be delivered is 24 cents per quart and 47 cents for two quarts. In local grocery stores milk will be 24 cents per quart. Whipping cream, formally 40 cents, is now 42 cents per quart and buttermilk, previously 19 cents, is now 20 cents per quart.

"The Sikeston Herald" December 20, 1951

BEDTIME CHRISTMAS EVE

Just a few more hours to wait! Here's the last glass of milk for the day —a Christmas cookie—then off to bed, to sleep and dream of that wonderful man with the red suit and white whiskers and his bulging pack of wonderful gifts! For all the bright-eyed believers in Santa Claus we wish the greatest gift of all . . . Good Health!

REISS DAIRY EMPLOYEES

Murl Greenlee	Roy Greenlee
Ray Lee	Ira Gene Hipes
Marvin Wallace	Louise Blackburn
Clyde Paylor	Bertis Blackburn
Walter McVeigh	Grace Carroll
Robert Atkinson	Emma Baker
Hurshel Bailey	Jamie K. Beakers
Merrill Hays	Ruth Marshall
Emory Oliver	Patricia Caldwell
Leslie Humes	Mary Lee Rainey
Hansel Duncan	Patsy Killian
Hugh Goode	Lucille Moore
Lenard McGee	Atlas Hatley, Jr.
Philip Cox	E. H. Spivey
Mildred Chartrau	James Saulters
Arabelle Cunningham	Harry Cummings
Elizabeth Wallace	Gordon Shy
Charlie Green	Wm. McCubbins
Ray Vick	Charles Eaker
H. C. Arnold	L. M. Standley
Bob Sides	John J. Reiss

SIKESTON MISSOURI *Reiss* DAIRY PASTEURIZED PRODUCTS

"The Daily Standard" September 22, 1953

Reiss Dairy Wins National Award

The Reiss Dairy has been awarded the bronze "Leader of Industry" award in recognition of its 100 per cent use of sanitary, Pure-Pak disposable milk cartons. In receiving this award, John J. Reiss owner of the Reiss Dairy, stated that this modern method of milk packaging has been in use in our dairy for four years. "Our customers" said Reiss, "appreciate the added convenience and sanitation of Pure-Pak disposable cartons, and their use has enabled us to greatly simplify and improve our dairy operation."

Pure-Pak milk containers are freshly made for each quart of milk they hold. They are formed, sterilized in molten paraffin, filled with milk and sealed automatically, without human handling. These modern milk containers are rapidly replacing the old fashioned glass milk bottle through the nation.

"The Daily Standard" December 17, 1954

Reiss Dairy Contest Has Great Response

As a supplement to the Dec. 13 issue of The Standard, Reiss Dairy had a full page of drawings to be colored by children of 12 years of age and under which are to be submitted to "Christmas Coloring Contest," e/o Reiss Dairy by mail and the postmark must be not later than next Monday, Dec. 20.

The response, according to L. M. Standley, has been overwhelming and a flood of colored drawings has already begun to pour in on the company but the contest is still open and if any boy or girl failed to get one of the coloring sheets, they may be obtained at Reiss Dairy, any Reiss dealer in the Sikeston area, or The Standard.

Contestants should be careful to make sure they sign their name, address, give their age and what grade he, or she, is in at school. Ten cash awards are being offered by Reiss for coloring the ten line drawings $10, $8, $5, $4, $3, and $2 for first to sixth places respectively, with $1 each being given for seventh, either, ninth, and tenth places.

You can use colored pencils, water colors or crayons and the awards will be based on neatness, accuracy, and appearance. A contestant can enter just as many drawings as he, or she, wishes, but only one award will be made to any one contestant. Any boy or girl, 12 years old or under is eligible except in families of employees of any dairy or The Standard.

January 1, 1955

Dear Friends —

Thanks for the pleasant memories of our f i n e relationship with all of you during the year 1954. It is a good feeling to look back on a year of progress, of fair dealing and fine friendship, which we hope will continue during 1955 — and for many years to come.

All of us at Reiss Dairy —

Wm. H. Shoulders	Atlas Hatley, Jr.	Doyne Chartrau
Harry Cummings	Gordon Shy	Louis Dillender
Charles Eaker	James Brase	Ronald Eaker
Cecil Joyce	E. H. Spivey	Frank Emerson
Murl Greenlee	James R. Lee	Marvin Wallace
Gene Hipes	Clyde Paylor	Robert Atkinson
J. M. Hays	Emory Oliver	Leslie Humes
Hansel Duncan		
Philip Cox	Hugh Goode	Lenard McGee
Thomas P. Duff	Bill Martin	Howard Manley
Harold Ragains	Charlie Green	Bill Warren
Elizabeth Wallace	Mildred Chartrau	A. Cunningham
Roy Greenlee	H. C. Arnold	Bob Sides
Patsy Killian	Don Bohanon	Verna Stout
Rosie Westbrook	Thelma Shipp	Iris Jean Earnest
Annie Troup	Melba Deal	Lillian Standley
Burl Heath	L. M. Standley	John J. Reiss

Wish you a HAPPY NEW YEAR!

"The Daily Standard" September 3, 1955

Reiss Dairy Cowbell Selected As Entry In Match Cover Contest

Match books from Reiss Dairy, Inc. (Cow Bell Dairy Bar), of Sikeston have been selected as an entry in the annual awards competition of the American match industry, the Match Industry Information Bureau has announced.

With 300,000 American business firms – one out of every 13 – putting messages on match covers, top advertising and marketing officials will select the outstanding examples in each of 46 industries. "Joshua" plaques and certificates will be awarded. The plaques are named for Joshua Pusey, inventor of match books.

The winners, chosen for effectiveness in doing a promotional job will also be pictured in a brochure to be distributed by the match industry, to serve as a guide for all who use match cover space.

"The Sikeston Herald" September 8, 1955

Reiss Dairy Announces Baby Contest

The Reiss Dairy of Sikeston, Mo., today announced that they are sponsoring a photographic contest to be known as the Reiss Dairy "Baby-of-the-Week." They have selected, as official photographers for this contest, which is to be run for an entire year, the TOPP Studios of Sikeston and Charleston.

Any youngster up to the age of 37 months is eligible. There is no entry fee or anything to buy and the contestant will be photographed by the TOPP Studio at no charge to the contestant or its family. The Reiss Dairy has contracted with the TOPP Studio to perform this service and the contestant and the family are under no obligation whatsoever.

To enter the contest, all this is necessary is to contact either the Reiss Dairy in Sikeston or the TOPP Studios in Sikeston or Charleston and the baby's name will be entered and an appointment made with the TOPP Studio to have the baby photographed. No other photographs will be accepted; only those made by the TOPP Studios of Sikeston and Charleston. Plan now to enter your child in the contest – call or write today.

"The Daily Standard" March 31, 1956
A Progressive Industry That Has Helped Sikeston's Progress

A pregnant idea in the mind of one man led to the beginning of the dairy industry in Sikeston. This one man was John J. Reiss, and the idea – well, he had seen the effects of unsafe, not-pasteurized milk on the health of his friends – and even relatives.

Back in 1932-33 when the Depression was at its worst, it took a lot of nerve to enter into a new business – very few customers, and no money. But he found a company that would sell him pasteurizing equipment and wait for its money. He bought the equipment, and how much milk do you think this equipment would pasteurize? Its capacity was 100 gallons, and the first batch Mr. Reiss pasteurized totaled 50 gallons. Do you think people ran over him trying to buy pasteurized milk? In that assumption you are mistaken for it took ten years to convince all his customers that pasteurized milk was THE safe milk to drink, and he discontinued the bottling of raw milk. As late as 1935, well-informed people in Sikeston were still asking, "Why pasteurize milk?"

Mr. Reiss started in business on his farm two miles east of Sikeston (now within the city limits) with a few cows and delivered milk in cans to the Dudley's Drug Store (where Bowman Drug Store now operates) and shortly thereafter a few friends and business acquaintances of his asked him to deliver milk in bottles to their homes. Of this original list of retail customers, three of them – believe it or not – still have Reiss Dairy Milk delivered to their homes. This is the beginning of a Sikeston industry that now employs about 50 persons and has an annual payroll that is well over $200,000.

With two high-school age daughters to deliver the milk (back there in the beginning), in the back seat of the family car – to a fleet of some 20 cars and trucks – that is how this idea of Mr. Reiss' has been accepted by people all over Southeast Missouri.

From the day back in 1932/33 when he processed the first milk in not-paid-for equipment in a building that had been at one time a chicken house to a modern brick steel and concrete building, located on U.S. Highway 61, South, you can readily see that some important changes have occurred in the dairy business in the last twenty-five years. Pasteurization and homogenization of milk – milk in paper cartons – refrigerated milk truck delivery – sixteen flavors of Jo-Kay Ice Cream and Sherbet – Grade "A" Dairy products – all these and many more improvements and innovations have made Reiss Dairy among the leaders in dairy operation.

Reiss Dairy Employees – Administrative: L. M. Standley, John J. Reiss and C. E. Redfearn. **Sales Department:** Burl E. Heath sales manager, Wm. H. Shoulders, Atlas Hatley Jr., Doyne Chartrau, Harry Cummings, Gordon Shy, Louis Dillender, Charles Eaker, Ronald Eaker, James Brase, Cecil "Ted" Joyce, E. H. Spivey, James Spivey, James Saulter, Bob Partin, Maurice Thompson, Gerald Kelley, Ernie Wallace, Wm. D. Harlow, Charles Wilburn, Donald Ray Bohannon. **Plant:** Ray Lee plant superintendent, Robert E. Atkinson, Phillip Cox, Thomas P. Duff Jr., Hansel Duncan, Hugh Goode, Charlie Green, Murl Greenlee, Roy Greenlee, Gene Hipes, Eddie Jolley, J. M. Hays, Leslie Humes, Lenard McGee, Howard Manley, Emory Oliver, Clyde Paylor, Clyde Nicholas, Marvin R. Wallace, Bob Sikes, H. C. Arnold. **Office:** Mildred

Chartrau manager, Arabelle Cunningham and Elizabeth Heuiser. **Cow Bell:** Verna Stout manager, Iris Jen Earnest, Thelma Shipp, Nancy Wilburn, Beverly Butler, Linda Jolley, Rosie Westbrook and Julie Renfro.

"The Sikeston Herald" May 17, 1956

THERE'S NO MAGIC TO MILK...

It's Simply The Finest Food On Earth . . . . .

Drinking milk probably won't make you well when you are sick, but milk will keep you healthy and strong — and you won't be as likely to get sick.

Milk — fresh milk — contains at least 273 different food values — some of which are not found in any other natural food. And milk is the most complete food, yet there is no magic in milk.

Drink FRESH Milk. Fresh vegetables begin to lose their fine, fresh flavor as soon as they are picked, so does Milk. That is the reason Reiss Dairy Milk is rushed from the Dairy to your Food Store (under mechanical refrigeration) —you must have Fresh Milk — with all the fine flavor and goodness.

Good Milk is clean milk — Milk from healthy cows — produced, processed and packaged in clean approved surroundings — all approved under a voluntary Grade A program.

Good Milk should be pasteurized — the extra — for your protection. Reiss Dairy has pasteurized milk for 25 years. Of course clarification, homogenization, and vacreation help maintain the flavor of good milk — Reiss Dairy has these too — but be sure the milk you buy is FRESH MILK — Milk from

Reiss DAIRY

DREAMY . . . . . CREAMY

STRAWBERRY COCONUT PIE

"The Daily Standard" June 5, 1957

Standley Opens Dairy Month Here by Appearing as Guest Speaker at the Kiwanis Club

Although dairying is only a small part of Southeast Missouri's agricultural economy, nationally it is the largest single source of cash income to the farmer, L. M. Standley told the Kiwanis Club at that group's regular meeting in the Dunn Hotel 'Tuesday night. Mr. Standley appeared as guest speaker as one of the features that will highlight the observance of Dairy Month, and was introduced by James M. Beaird, manager of the Chamber of Commerce, which is sponsoring the Dairy Month program locally.

All the milk produced in the United States in a single year, said Standle3y, would form a river 3,000 miles long, three feet deep and 500 feet wide. And the use of milk is increasing, he said. Last year the volume of milk used was up 7.5 per cent over the previous year. A peculiar fact is that the eight larger milk distributing companies of the nation are going into a world-wide milk production and distribution program and, right now, a seventh of one of the major milk company's business is done in the Orient.

The trend, the speaker continued, is for more and more consolidation with smaller independent dairies giving way to the hug organizations.

But the speaker's topic was "Dairying and What It Means to Sikeston," and, getting down to local conditions, Mr. Standley gave what, to some at least, were some surprising figures as to the importance of Reiss Dairy, or which Mr. Standley is manager, to the economy of this immediate area.

The company, he said, last year spent $91,000 for paper items, such as containers, ice cream cups, etc. After the new paper conversion plant of Potlatch Forests, Inc. is in operation, he continued, Reiss will buy its containers locally if they can provide them. These paper containers come to the company 'knocked down' and are assembled, waxed, filled and sealed by special machines they have for that purpose.

On the cost of delivering milk, Standley said it costs about five cents for the container alone and 12.1 cents per mile to operate the milk trucks. To deliver a quart of milk to the customer's door costs between 6 and 7 cents per quart. Handling milk is also expensive. For each 100 pounds it costs $3.82, about midway between the cost in Memphis and St. Louis.

Milk for the local dairy is secured from modernly equipped dairies where the milk is handled under most rigid specifications. As a matter of fact, he pointed out, from the time the automatic milkers are used to milk the cows until the customer breaks the seal on the container, no human hands touch the fluid; in fact, the milk isn't even seen. It is conveyed from the milkers to cooling tanks and from there to tank trucks and to the dairy in glass lined pipes and is never exposed to the air at any time.

There are some 50 employees in the plant here and, last year, salaries amounted to $269,000. In addition, the company paid local taxes, incenses, etc., amounting to $9,840; paid out $677,000 for milk and $34,000 for miscellaneous supplies. Altogether, about a million dollars, most of which was put into circulation right here.

In addition to the expenses of the dairy itself, each producer from whom Reiss buys milk has an average expense of between $25,000 and $30,000 for equipment, modern dairy barns, cooling tanks, etc.

Following Mr. Standley's talk, Mr. Beaird announced he had been informed that Potlach Forests, Inc. is seriously considering making Sikeston the headquarters for its dairy division which, he said, would certainly mean an increase in the size of the plant here from the original plans.

"The Sikeston Herald" August 29, 1957

Death Takes John J. Reiss

Founder of Dairy Here Had Been in Failing Health Many Months

Sikeston lost one of its most valued citizens and most prominent businessmen at early Wednesday when death came to John J. Reiss at the Missouri Delta Community Hospital, where he had been a patient for several weeks. He had been in failing health for many months.

The body is at the Welsh Funeral Home, where it will be in state until time for funeral services which will be conducted by his pastor, the Rev. E. D. Owen, at the First Baptist Church at 3 o'clock Friday afternoon.

Mr. Reiss was a native of Floraville, Ill. Having been born there Nov. 4, 1877, the son of the late Frank J. and Syvilla Ann Reiss. After spending some years in Flat River, Mo., Mr. Reiss came to Sikeston community in 1909 and operated a farm near Matthews for ten years. In 1919 he bought a farm in what is now the eastern part of Sikeston and there in 1928 he established the Reiss Farm Dairy. He later sold his farm, moving his business and residence into Sikeston.

Mr. Reiss married the former Miss Etta Sellards on Jan. 24, 1910. She died Sept. 20, 1947. Two daughters survive. They are Miss Audrey Reiss of Dallas, Texas, and Lillian (Mrs. Lonnie M.) Standley of Sikeston. Also surviving are two granddaughters, Jo Ellen and Kay Standley of Sikeston; a sister, Mrs. Kate Petry of Belleville, Ill., and three brothers, Louis P. Reiss of Dallas, Texas, William M. Reiss of Belleville, Ill., and George Reiss of Freeburg, Ill. A sister and a brother are deceased.

Every worthwhile community effort received the support and active participation of Mr. Reiss. He had been a member of the Baptist Church during practically all of his adult life, was a former superintendent of the Sunday School of the First Baptist Church in Sikeston and had long been a member of the church's board of deacons. He also served as a member of the building committee in charge of the erection of the church's educational building. Mr. Reiss was a member of the Masonic Shrine and Scottish Rite orders. He was a former president of the Scott County Farm Bureau and took a lively interest in all movements to benefit the farming industry. He is a former president of the Sikeston National Farm Loan Association and a member of the board of directors of the Sikeston Production Credit Association, also a director of the New Madrid County Farmers Mutual Fire Insurance Co. During World War II, he served as chairman of the Scott County Red Cross chapter. Several years ago, Mr. Reiss promoted and headed the Miner Community Club.

Mr. Reiss' greatest material monument is the Reiss Dairy, which he founded in 1928, of which he and his son-in-law L. M. Standley, have managed so successfully that it is now one of Sikeston's principal industries. The Reiss Dairy in 1940 began producing the first homogenized milk sold in this area. In 1949 the dairy moved into its beautiful and commodious building on Highway 61 and in the south part of Sikeston, making the Cow Bell milk bar and light lunch café a part of the business. Also, at that time it began producing ice cream under the Jo-Kay label.

In 1951 the Reiss Dairy voluntarily accepted the provisions of the United States Public Health Milk Ordinance and Code with the supervision of the Scott County Health Department. In May of this year the City of Sikeston adopted a Grade A ordinance.

The Reiss Dairy now employs 50 people with an annual payroll of over $250,000 and last year paid over a half-million dollars to local producers for milk supplied by their dairy herds. With a record like that left by John J. Reiss, his place in Sikeston will be difficult to fill.

"The Daily Sikeston" January 12, 1959

"The Daily Standard" December 8, 1967

AND DON'T FORGET

REISS QUALITY CHEKD EGG NOG IS NOW AVAILABLE- AND WHEN WE SAY AVAILABLE WE MEAN YOUR FOOD STORE HAS IT. YES, REISS QUALITY CHEKD EGG NOG IS AVAILABLE-

KEEP A QUART OR TWO IN YOUR REFRIGERATOR ALL THE TIME-THE CHILDREN JUST LOVE REISS QUALITY CHEKD EGG NOG- YOUR GUESTS WILL SAY IT'S THE BEST REFRESHMENT EVER.

REISS DAIRY INC.

SIKESTON, MO.

EGG NOG IS JUST EGG NOG UNLESS IT'S REISS QUALITY CHEKD

"The Daily Standard" March 14, 1970
Sale of Dairy Imminent

Lonnie M. Standley, president of Reiss Dairy, Highway 61 South, indicated today an announcement of the sale of Reiss Dairy was imminent. He said another company's representative was expected in Sikeston today and would make an announcement.

"The Daily Standard" March 16, 1970

Mr. and Mrs. L. M. Standley, owners of Reiss Dairy, announced today the sale of the business to Turner Dairies of Covington, Tenn.

"The Sikeston Standard Democrat" October 27, 2003
Reiss Dairy History as Told by Lonnie Standley

John Jacob Reiss founded the Reiss Dairy in Sikeston, Missouri. He started selling milk from his own cows to neighbors and then to local retailers. That led to starting his own dairy and becoming a retailer himself. "About the year 1940, when Reiss Dairy was located in a frame building at 523 East Malone Avenue in Sikeston, processed milk products were packaged in glass – that is all products except butter which was packaged in folded cardboard one-pound cartons."

"Reiss Diary packaged processed milk in three sizes of bottles – ½ pint, pint, and quart sizes. The bottles were purchased in shipments when needed by the truckloads from glass bottle manufacturers. I can remember only two manufacturers – Owens-Illinois Glass and Liberty Glass Co. All manufacturers would apply sizes and the Dairy trade name on the bottle. We selected red as the color of this application. The name was more or less permanent, depending on the caustic washing material used and the wear and tear of constant use. One of the manufacturers told us we could place an advertising message on the opposite side of the bottle so here is where the applied verses began."

"We decided we would ask our customers to help us advertise Reiss Dairy products. We placed a paid advertisement in the twice a week Sikeston Standard. We placed this advertisement only once at a probable cost of less than $10. The size of the advertisement was two columns by eight includes for the single insertion. The advertisement read something like this: Do you like to doodle or write ditties? Write your choice and bring it to the Reiss Dairy Office. When you see your work placed on a Reiss Dairy Milk Bottle, bring the bottle to our Reiss Dairy Office and collect $1.00 cash. Reiss Dairy 523 East Malone Avenue, Sikeston, Missouri."

"This advertisement brought very slow results, but gradually interest increased and poems came in – in large numbers. As we placed orders for new bottles, the poems were changed and new poems were selected. We kept this program in effect until we changed milk packaging from glass to paper which was in 1949 when we were in our new building at 526 S. Main Street in Sikeston."

"I have no idea how many verses we received, but the ladies working in our office really enjoyed making the selections of verses when new orders for milk bottles were placed. They placed all verses as received in a big box and stored in a safe place. When we began packaging milk in paper, we had milk bottles to destroy. We hauled milk bottles to the trash heap – truckloads of them. One lady told us that Reiss Dairy milk bottles are now valued at $150 on the Internet.

"The Cow Bell" Dairy Bar

"The Sikeston Herald" December 30, 1948

Reiss Dairy to Open "Cow Bell" Saturday At New Plant on Highway 61, South

Reiss Dairy will open its new milk bar – the Cow Bell – Saturday morning when that portion of the new dairy plant is opened to the public on Highway 61, South. The opening of the Cow Bell will precede the formal opening of the entire dairy plant by about two weeks, Reiss Dairy officials state. Original plans to open the modern plant January 1 have been delayed but the Cow Bell will ring in the new year on schedule with door swinging wide for the first time.

Located at the northwest corner of the new plant, the Cow Bell is attractively furnished for the convenience and comfort of both patrons and employees. A half-acre parking lot on the north side of the building will add to the convenience of customers and provide improved service of Reiss Dairy products.

Inside the milk bar tables have been placed opposite three horseshoe counters. The interior is completely modern in design and equipment, with various shades of brown blending into a series of provoking patterns.

Located in the beautiful light buff brick Reiss Dairy plant, the Cow Bell will feature Reiss Dairy products and Jo-Kay ice cream – a tasty product named after the two daughters of Plant Manager and Mrs. L. M. Standley. The Dow bell will be operated by Mr. and Mrs. B. D. Blackburn, both of whom have had several years' experience in preparing and dispensing food and fountain drinks.

Although the new plant will not be ready for inspection by the public for two weeks, Reiss Dairy officials are extending an invitation for all to visit the Cow Bell when it opens Saturday.

Final installations and tests for new equipment have delayed opening the entire plant. The futuristic plant has been planned to conform to requirements of the U. S. Public Health Ordinance and the plans were examined by the Missouri State Board of Health before the building program began.

In the areas where milk is processed, the walls are of light cream glazed tile and the floors of white concrete. The ceiling is aluminum enameled white. Sufficient light has been provded to appropriately name the plant "Sunshine Dairy."

Edgar Stephens & Sons of Cairo were contractors for the building with Webb Electric Co;. and T. L. Davey respectively installing electrical and plumbing fixtures. R. Paul Buchmueller was architect for the "Sunshine Dairy," where equipment is of the latest design and where dairy products will be processed in a manner conducive to better health for the people of Sikeston and the district.

"The Sikeston Herald" December 30, 1948

THE

COW

BELL

"MILK BAR"

HIGHWAY 61, SOUTH

at Reiss Dairy's New Plant

Featuring Reiss Dairy Products and Jo-Kay Ice Cream

— Stop and Eat at the "COW BELL —

* ★ BEVERAGES
* ★ MILK SHAKES AND MALTS
* ★ SUNDAES
* ★ PARFAITS
* ★ ICE CREAM FLAVORS
* ★ SANDWICHES
* ★ SALADS
* ★ SANDWICH-SALAD COMBINATIONS

THE **COW BELL**

MR. AND MRS. B. D. BLACKBURN, Managers

Telephone No. 349   Highway 61, South

"The Daily Standard" January 4, 1949

'Cow Bell' Has Large Opening Day Crowd

The opening of the Reiss Dairy new "Cow Bell" on Highway 61 S. was proclaimed "very successful" today by employees of the new establishment. Mr. and Mrs. B. D. Blackburn, managers of the "Cow Bell" said they were very busy on opening day, Saturday, Jan. 1, and were well pleased with the results.

The "Cow Bell" features the products of the Reiss Dairy and Jo-Kay ice cream. "Grand Opening" of the dairy's entire new plant will not take place for about two weeks yet, company officials reported. The "Cow Bell" is open from 10 o'clock in the morning until 10 o'clock at night.

"The Sikeston Herald" January 6, 1949

Opening of "Cow Bell" Attended by Hundreds

Hundreds of people of Sikeston and neighboring communities were patrons of the town's newest eating place, the "Cow Bell," last Saturday and the days following. The attendance on opening day – Saturday – was beyond the expectations of the owners and operators. In fact, a number of the personnel stated that there were times when certain of the foods offered were exhausted. It was stated that in addition to a host of Sikeston folks who have patronized the "Cow Bell," patrons were seen from Portageville, Lilbourn, New Madrid, Charleston, Morehouse, St. Louis, and other communities.

The "Cow Bell" is located in the new building of the Reiss Dairy at the southeast corner of Sikeston and is being operated under lease by Mr. and Mrs. D. B. Blackburn.

While the fine dairy building is ready for occupancy, it will not be formally opened for approximately a month. New machinery is now being installed under the direction of an expert machinist from St. Louis and other machinery from the present processing plant on Malone Avenue must be moved to the new building. All this moving and installing takes considerable time and the moving is complicated by the fact that the production and distribution of the dairy's products must be continued without interruption.

Thanks a Million

Your Response to the Opening of

The Cow Bell

Was beyond Our Expectations

We will continue to try to serve the best in
Dairy Foods at reasonable prices

SIKESTON
MISSOURI
Reiss
DAIRY
PASTEURIZED
PRODUCTS

"The Daily Standard" January 18, 1949

Why "The Cow Bell"?

The name *Cow Bell* (Reiss Dairy Milk Bar) originated from a real cow bell that has been handed down through the family until now this particular bell is in possession of the fifth generation from the original owner. It is a family treasure. No more fitting tribute could be given to the ancestors of the present owners than to name the "Cow Bell" after those pioneers who long ago realized the food value of milk. Every family had one or more cows, even though in most cases there was no enclosed pasture to keep them. To insure finding the cows when milking time came, a cow bell was placed around the neck of the lead cow. The ringing of the cow bell could be heard for miles.

To those pioneers, the sound of the cow bell meant good, wholesome and nourishing milk — so necessary in those days for strength and good health. To you, the present generation, the "Cow Bell" means a place that serves the best in good wholesome dairy foods — so necessary even today for good health.

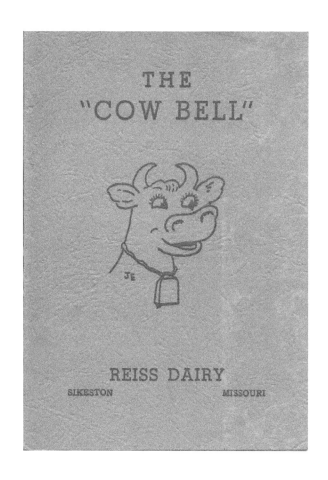

FEATURING REISS DAIRY PRODUCTS AND JO-KAY ICE CREAM

Specials

Banana Split	.35
Peach a la Mode	.20
Ice Cream Cone	.05 and .10
Ice Cream Bowl	.20
any flavor	

Ice Cream Flavors

Vanilla
Strawberry
Black Walnut
Chocolate-Marsh Ripple
Chocolate
Fruit Salad
Raspberry Ripple

Sandwiches

All Sandwiches Toasted with Reiss Dairy Butter

Cowbell	.30	Pimiento Cheese	.25
Ham (toasted or bun)	.30	American Cheese	.25
Ham Salad	.30	Tomato and Lettuce	.20
Chicken Salad	.35	Ham and Cheese	.40
Tuna Salad	.35	Peanut Butter and Jelly	.20

Salads
a la carte

Tuna Filled Tomato	.40	Pear and Cottage Cheese	.35
Chic. Salad Filled Tomato	.40	Pineapple and Cot. Cheese	.35
Cottage Cheese	.30	Peach and Cottage Cheese	.35
Lettuce	.25	Cottage Cheese	.25
thousand island dressing			

Sandwich-Salad Combination

Ham—any fruit salad combination	.50
Ham Salad—any fruit salad combination	.50
Chicken Salad—any fruit salad combination	.55
Tuna—any fruit salad combination	.55
Ham-Cheese—any fruit salad combination	.60
Tomato-Lettuce—any fruit salad combination	.40

Beverages

Milk	.07
Chocolate Milk	.07
Lactic Buttermilk	.05
Special Buttermilk	.08
Bireley's Orangeade	.05
Hot Chocolate	.10
Coffee	.05
Fresh Orangeade	.05 and .10
Fresh Limeade	.05 and .10
Fresh Lemonade	.05 and .10
Coca-Cola	.05 and .10
Root Beer	.05
Hot Tea	.05
Phosphates	.05 and .10
cherry, lemon, strawberry	

Milk Shakes and Malts

Milk Shakes	.20
vanilla, chocolate, cherry, pineapple, strawberry	
Malted Milks	.25
vanilla, chocolate, cherry, pineapple, strawberry	
Ice Cream Sodas	.20
vanilla, chocolate, cherry, pineapple, strawberry	

Sundaes

Hot Fudge	.25	Butterscotch	.25
Hot Butterscotch	.25	Fruit Salad	.25
Milk Chocolate	.25	Strawberry	.25
Marshmallow	.25	Pineapple	.25
Chocolate Marshmallow	.25	Cherry	.25

Parfaits

Milk Chocolate	.25	Butterscotch	.25
Marshmallow	.25	Strawberry	.25
Chocolate Marshmallow	.25	Pineapple	.25
Cherry	.25		

Big Gob Strawberry Ice Cream Cups

Tuesday, January 3, 2012

Hi Steve,

About the 'Big Gob' – what an unappealing name for a food product! I don't remember it exactly, but I think it was "catchy" packaging for a small cup or so of ice cream. It must have been a Reiss Dairy product. Daddy didn't start using other products until the soft custard craze started in the late 50's. At that point, he bought the custard base which he thought was awful. The design on the lid was drawn by my sister Jo when she was in grade school – maybe 10 or 11 – which would place the date as late 40's or 1950 since she was born in 1938. I remember the drawing, and actually may have the original in the dairy memorabilia. Steve, I took the things I sent you for the Dairy book from that cache, and would be glad to share the rest of the things at some point.

Let me know if there is anything I can do to help.

Love, Katy

Investment in Scouting is Money in the Bank of Young Manhood

THE SIKESTON HERALD

PART TWO—Pages 9-16 | SIKESTON, MISSOURI, THURSDAY, FEBRUARY 3, 1949 | VOL. 49—NO. 5

Formal Opening of Reiss Dairy Plant

Buildings and Equipment to Be Inspected by Public Saturday

Beginning Saturday, February 5, and continuing until next Tuesday evening will be the formal opening of the new Reiss Dairy processing plant and equipment.

From 1 to 5 o'clock Saturday afternoon, the new plant will be open for visitation and inspection of the general public.

On Sunday, from 2 to 5 p.m., the plant will be open to merchants of the district served by the Reiss Dairy.

Monday evening, special guests will be suppliers to the Dairy, including wholesalers, jobbers and their representatives, dairy owners and managers, of the district.

On Tuesday at 10 a.m. a special meeting for milk producers will be held at the Sikeston Armory, at which time an outstanding speaker will address the group.

The Cow Bell, a cafe specializing in dairy products foods, which is housed in the Reiss Dairy building and has already proven to be a popular place for those wanting light lunches and snacks, was formally opened January 1, with Mr. and Mrs. B. D. Blackburn as managers.

A Dream Come True

The new building and equipment of the Reiss Dairy is literally a dream come true. Its owners and managers have long wanted a building of such attractiveness as to be an ornament to the progressive community in which it is located and of such size as to house a business that had long since outgrown its former location.

After many months of inspecting other modern dairy processing plants and planning the new plant here, the new Reiss Dairy building was begun just a year ago on a three-acre tract of land on Highway 61 in the southeastern part of Sikeston.

A Story of Progress

The history of Reiss Dairy is one of progress. A few of the "firsts" that can be attributed to advances made by the firm in the dairy field are:

1. First dairy to process and sell pasteurized milk in the Sikeston area.
2. First dairy in Sikeston to make cottage cheese, butter and chocolate milk.
3. First dairy in Sikeston to process and sell homogenized milk. In fact the first dairy in rural Missouri to homogenize milk.
4. First dairy in Sikeston to service outlying towns with dairy products.
5. First dairy in Sikeston to use all stainless steel equipment in processing dairy products.

Small Beginning

Reiss Dairy has grown from a small beginning when back about 1928, John J. Reiss started delivering a few quarts of milk to stores and homes in Sikeston. At that time many people in Sikeston had their own cows or purchased their dairy needs from their neighbors. The first Reiss Dairy plant was a building on the farm about 12 feet square which was later destroyed by fire. It was replaced by one slightly larger. This one in turn was replaced by a still larger plant located on the farm. This building was about 18 feet by 30 feet and had a cold storage room built in it. It was in this building that Mr. Reiss installed his first pasteurizer about 1931. Business grew steadily, even during the depression years, and other dairy products were processed—butter, cottage cheese, chocolate milk and buttermilk.

In 1935, Mr. Reiss decided that a dairy plant in Sikeston would be an asset to his business and a convenience for the customers, so he purchased a restaurant building at 523 E. Malone Avenue. This building was remodeled and an addition made thereto so that there would be enough room for a dairy plant, cold storage room and office. In the years 1936-41 this building was enlarged several times to make room for a growing business. Larger and more efficient equipment was installed as time went on until Reiss Dairy became one of the largest processors in this area.

Trade territory was added until Reiss Dairy trucks gave daily delivery service to cities as far away as Caruthersville, East Prairie and Chaffee. Six trucks are now used to deliver dairy products in Sikeston and other towns. Six routes are necessary to pick up milk from farms, much of this milk going back over the same roads used to haul the milk to the dairy plant.

Years of Planning

The new Reiss Dairy plant is a result of years of planning. New equipment was placed on order for the new plant as early as 1945. The size of the plant, the layout of the various rooms and departments was seriously studied for several months before the architect started work. Preliminary drawings of floor plans were made by the dozens, but finally after consultation with dairy engineers and the architect, R. Paul Buchmueller, a floor plan was made that met the enthusiastic response of the owners. It embraced two buildings with about 12,000 square feet of floor space, the larger building housing the dairy bar, offices and dairy plant, the smaller building being a heating plant building.

The dairy plant building is designed so the two offices and the dairy bar occupy the entire front of the building with the dairy plant to the rear.

The central office is just to the right of the front entrance as you enter the building. A window has been installed for the convenience of the customers so that business may be transacted with a minimum of confusion. Desks and filing cabinets are conveniently arranged for office personnel and a lavatory and a cloakroom are included in the space allotted for the office. A smaller private office for the owners is located adjacent to the central office. The offices and "Cow Bell" are heated by a hot air circulating unit in winter and cooled by cold air in summer. Another feature of the office arrangement is a specially designed area where salesmen may check in to the office and complete their reports.

Sanitary Processing Rooms

In the center of the dairy building is a large processing and packaging room. This is an area covering some 2500 square feet. The walls are glazed tile, the ceiling aluminum enameled white and the floors are white concrete. Ample floor drains have been provided to care for surface water on the floor. All doors are steel enameled white. This room houses dozens of pieces of equipment, both large and small, necessary to the processing of dairy products. A large milk receiving room is located at the rear of the building on the south side. In this room milk is received from the farms, weighed, graded and tested, the empty cans are washed and returned to the farms. A large machinery room is located in the rear in which is located refrigeration machinery so necessary in processing milk as well as power and lighting panel boards. Along the north side of the building are two insulated milk and ice cream storage rooms. Provision has been made so that dairy products can be easily loaded on trucks for delivery to stores and consumers. Adequate shower, locker and toilet facilities have been provided for plant personnel. The entire building is of fireproof material. The front of the building is cream colored brick and rear faced with red brick. The roof is steel supported and is insulated with fire-proof material.

A driveway entirely around the building is used by trucks delivering milk to the building and loading for delivery to the trade. A half acre parking lot on the north side of the building is for use of customers of the "Cow Bell."

The Men Behind the Plant

Business institutions like the Reiss Dairy and the modern plant just completed could not exist unless someone caused them to exist. In the case of the Reiss Dairy and its buildings and equipment, the people who caused them to exist for this week's inspection and for future service to a growing community were John J. Reiss and his son-in-law, Lonnie M. Standley, owners and managers of the dairy business which bears the name of the former and its founder.

Mr. Reiss is a native of Illinois, having been born near Belleville in that state in 1877. His dairy experience also began in that city and he was later connected with dairies at Floraville, Ill., and Flat River, Mo. Other preparation for his successful business experience were courses of study in dairying at Illinois and Missouri State Universities.

In 1909 Mr. Reiss came to Southeast Missouri and for ten years he operated the W. H. Andrews farm near Matthews now owned by Mr. and Mrs. Oscar Carroll. In 1919 he bought a farm east of Sikeston, where he lived until six years ago, moving to Sikeston in 1942.

In 1910 Mr. Reiss married Miss Etta Sellards, who passed away in 1947. Their two daughters are Lillian (Mrs. L. M. Standley) of Sikeston and Miss Audrey Reiss of Phoenix, Ariz.

In addition to his busy life as a farmer and dairyman, Mr. Reiss has always had time to give to the civic and religious interests of his community. He has long been an official member of the First Baptist church of Sikeston and has served as its Sunday school superintendent. He has served as vice-president and later as president of the Scott County Farm Bureau, as chairman of the Scott County Red Cross and in many other helpful capacities.

Mr. Standley is a native of Southeast Missouri, having been born near Poplar Bluff in 1907. He attended Washington University in St. Louis and State College at Cape Girardeau, receiving his degree as Bachelor of Science at the latter school. For several years he taught school in St. Louis county, coming to Sikeston and joining Mr. Reiss in the dairy business in 1935.

In 1934 Mr. Standley was married to Miss Lillian Reiss and they have two daughters, Jo Ellen, 10, and Kay, 7. It is for the two girls that one of the products of the Reiss Dairy, "Jo-Kay Ice Cream," is named.

Mr. Standley, too, has taken a lively interest in community affairs of his home district. Being a member of the Methodist church, he has served as chairman of the official board and as Sunday school superintendent of the Sikeston church and at present is a member of the board of stewards. In 1938 he was president of the Kiwanis Club of Sikeston and is now one of the leaders in that service club. In 1944 he served as president of the Sikeston Chamber of Commerce. In Boy Scout work he has been a prominent leader, as he has in many other civic endeavors.

New, Modern Home of the Reiss Dairy

THE REISS DAIRY OPENING SCHEDULE

Saturday, February 5, 1 to 5 p.m., for general public.

Sunday, February 6, 2 to 5 p.m., for merchants of patronizing territory.

Monday evening, February 7, for suppliers, including wholesalers, jobbers, their representatives, dairy owners and managers of this community.

Tuesday, Feb. 8, at 10 a.m., at the Sikeston Armory, for milk producers.

Owners and Managers of the Reiss Dairy

JOHN J. REISS

LONNIE M. STANDLEY

West Inside View of the Cow Bell

East Inside View of the Cow Bell

REA OFFICIALS ATTEND NATIONAL CONVENTION IN NEW YORK THIS WEEK

Officials of the Scott-New Madrid-Mississippi Electric Cooperative left last Friday morning for New York City to attend the national convention of Rural Electric Administration cooperatives being held at Hotel Commodore in that city this week.

Those attending from the district cooperative include H. M. Zaricor of Sikeston, manager; Judge Elon Proffer of Matthews, president; Mrs. Proffer, Mr. and Mrs. R. J. Stroud of Matthews; Jim Spradling of Kewanee, L. B. Mayer and Roscoe Russell of Dexter, and Louis Albrecht of Illmo. They are expected home next Monday.

Dairy Bar Is Distinctly Modern

The dairy bar, named the "Cow Bell," has indirect lighting with acoustical fire proof ceiling, and plastered walls have been painted or papered attractive colors. The floor is terrazzo. The counter is a bay type that seats 36 persons. Five tables with chairs near the wall of the room complete the seating arrangement. The fountain is an island type which permits the operators to work all around the fountain equipment without interferring with the customers.

The fountain equipment is all stainless steel, table and counter tops are tan linen formica. At one end of the "Cow Bell" two ice cream cabinets and a dairy display case have been installed for "carry out" business. Provision has been made for curb service at a later date. A kitchen for preparation of food and dishwashing has been provided for, as well as two public rest rooms and a locker room for the fountain operators. All refrigeration machinery necessary to operate the fountain are in separate rooms which eliminates much of the noise.

DESIGNS SOLICITED IN EASTER SEAL CONTEST

St. Louis, Mo.—High school art students throughout Missouri have been invited to compete in the 1949 Easter Seal Design contest, for which local, state and national prizes are offered by the Crippled Children's Societies and Communities who use the Easter Seal as a symbol of their service to handicapped children. The winning design in the national contest will appear on more than two billion seals which will be sold in 1951 throughout the nation.

The Missouri Society for Crippled Children and Adults Inc. offers a first award of a $100 Savings Bond and a second award of a $50 U. S. Savings Bond for winning designs in the Missouri contest. Entries for this must be received by the Missouri Society at 3714 Washington Boulevard, St. Louis, by March 30.

Judges for the Easter Seal Design contest in Missouri include D. R. Fitzpatrick, noted cartoonist of the St. Louis Post-Dispatch, James Harmon, head of the Art Department, University City Public Schools, and W. Smart, art director of D'Arcy Advertising Company, St. Louis.

Winners of the Missouri contest will be entered in the national contest, sponsored by the National Society for Crippled Children and Adults Inc. The first award of the National Society is a $500 art scholarship for one year; second award is a $200 art scholarship for one term; third award is a $100 U. S. Savings Bond or the equivalent in art lessons; fourth award is a $50 U. S. Savings Bond or art lessons.

In addition, many County Crippled Children's Societies or Committees are sponsoring local Easter Seal design contests which will close March 21.

COTTON QUOTAS NOT TO BE BASED ON 1949 PLANTINGS

The House Agriculture Committee has agreed that 1949 cotton plantings not be used in figuring production quotas.

Any farm on which cotton was not planted in 1947 or 1948 shall be regarded as having a 1948 planted acreage equal to the 1942 farm acreage allotment.

Quotas are expected to be ordered for the 1950 crop, however, because of steadily increasing cotton supplies.

Reiss Dairy Products

Metal lids for 8- and 15-ounce glass jars of Creamed Cottage Cheese. Below is a 12-ounce cottage cheese jar which could also hold that much Budweiser!

Here's also a glass jar which once held whipping cream, long before the days of aerosol cans. Its paper label did not survive repeated washing.

March 15, 1962

December 8, 1967

Hi Steve,

We were in Sikeston at a reunion a few weeks ago and I was approached by a woman who said she had an ice cream carton that she would send me. She did and I am forwarding it to you. Do you have such a thing? Very strange to me — used I assume. Why keep it? It's in beautiful condition, isn't it, for something that probably had ice cream in it — fudge ripple! (I remember it well! Good stuff!)

So good to see you and Grant and visit for a while. It was a lovely evening with the Freeman's. We hope you and Diane visit us soon. Are you coming East? Grant looks great and so happy.

> Love,
> Katy

Advertising

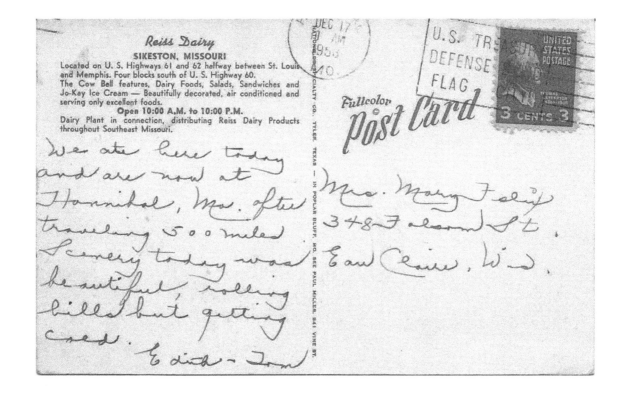

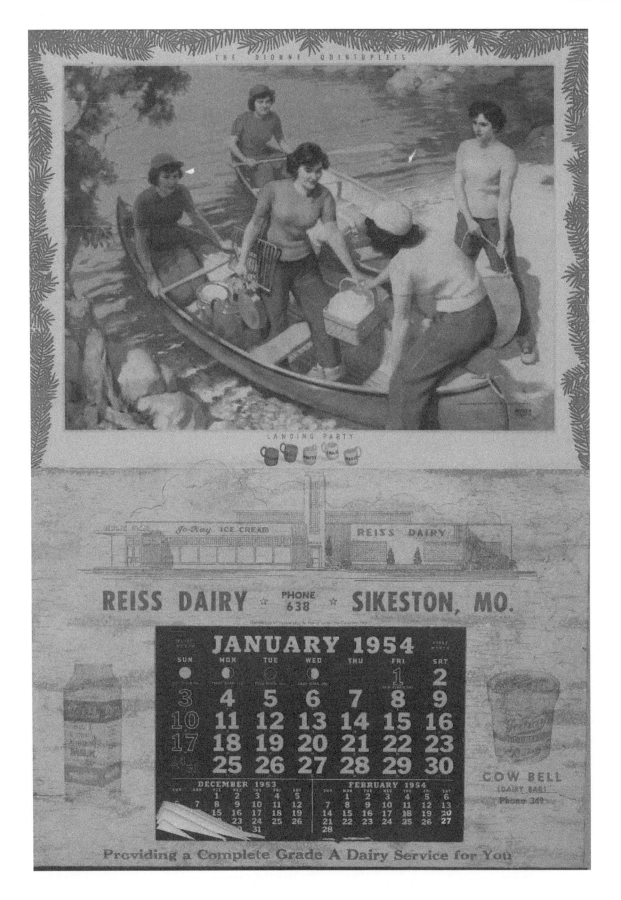

Reiss Dairy Cowbell Selected As Entry In Match Cover Contest

Match books from Reiss Dairy, Inc. (Cow Bell Dairy Bar), of Sikeston have been selected as an entry in the annual awards competition of the American match industry, the Match Industry Information Bureau has announced.

With 300,000 American business firms — one out of every 13 —putting messages on match covers, top advertising and marketing officials will select the outstanding examples in each of 46 industries. "Joshua" plaques and certificates will be awarded. The plaques are named for Joshua Pusey, inventor of match books.

The winners, chosen for effectiveness in doing a promotional job will also be pictured in a brochure to be distributed by the match industry, to serve as a guide for all who use match cover space.

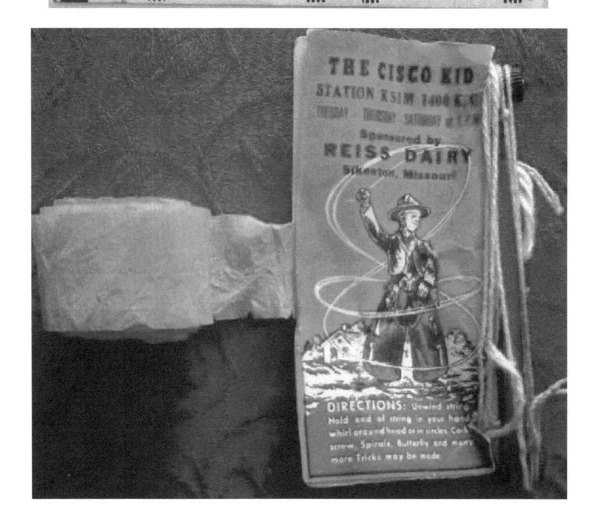

Clipboard and pencils for taking orders.

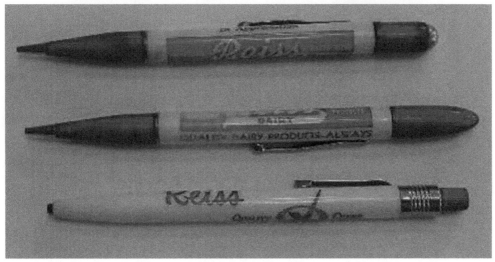

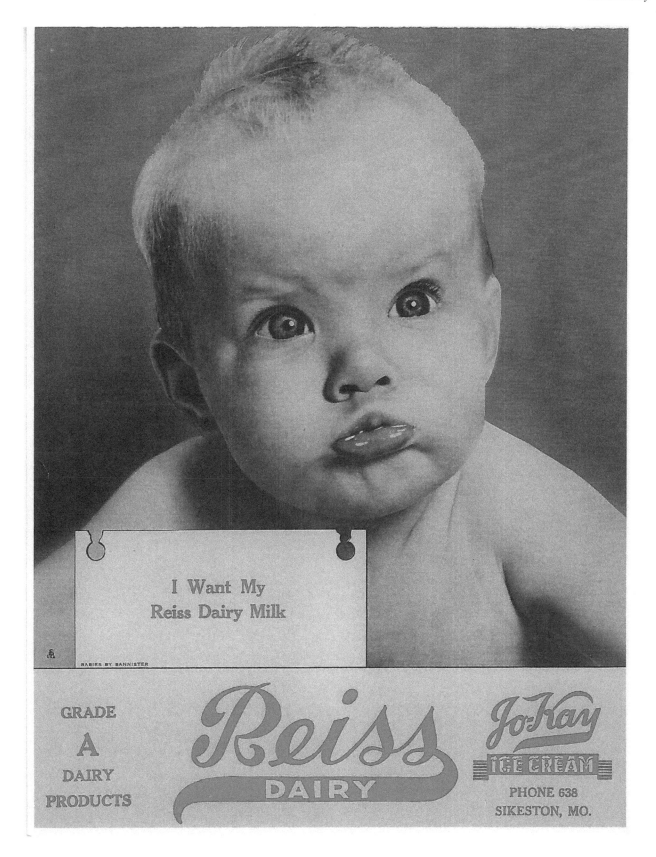

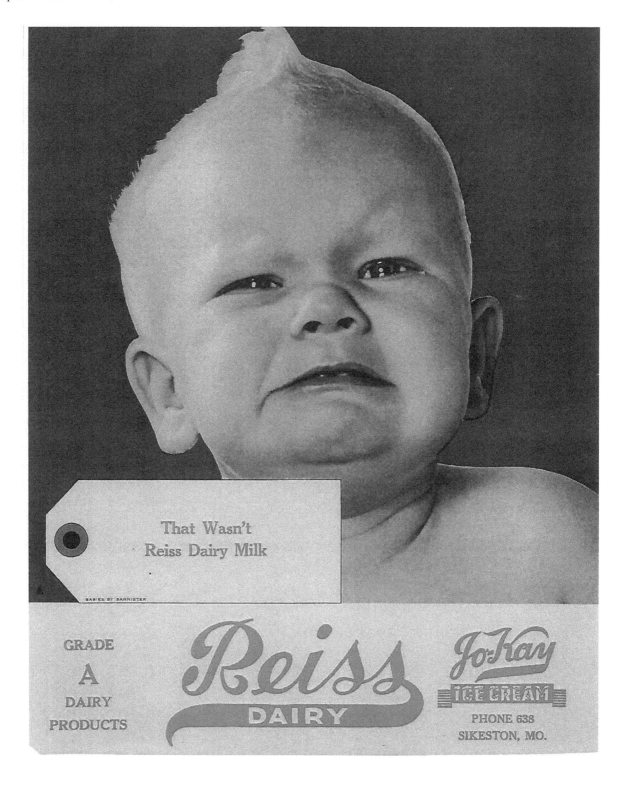

Reiss Dairy Equipment

Two Reiss Dairy milk cans and a cream can all painted by Bonnie Allen. A mold for freezing ice cream on a stick.

This photograph was taken about 1940 in the Malone ave. plant.

1. Mr John J Reiss is shown at the left

2. The round tank in the foreground is a 50 gallon Univat by Cherry-Burrell — the first piece of equipment ever purchased, made of Stainless steel interior and painted steel exterior.

3. The milk/cream separator was one where we attached a motor so it did not have to be operated manually.

4. The oblong vat on legs is a. Cottage cheese vat. The skim milk from the cream separator is emptying into the Cheese vat. The Cream is flowing into a 10 gallon can.

5. In the output background, a milk bottling machine is operating. You can see quart bottles full of milk

Thanks for being my #1 Costomer,
and friend during the many years
I kept those Dairy trucks rolling.
It was a very good time in my
Life and Susiness. Most if my
Sucesss was due to your patonage.
thanks
G.A. (Chick) Reynolds

Reiss Dairy Milk Bottle Poems
by Author

Here are poems and authors found on eBay and elsewhere so far. SWR denotes my personal collection of milk bottles. The underlined authors identify 28 additional poems found since the first edition of this book was published. Dare we say that book brought more bottles and poems to the surface???

Co-owner Lonnie Standley's favorite poem was "Fuzzy Wuzzy" by Mary Jane Farris.

Audrey Aldrich

Once there was a little girl who lived across the street,
She wasn't feeling very well and didn't know what to eat,
And when I told her of Reiss' Dairy Milk and she drank it every day,
Now she's feeling very well and proud of it today.

Merlin Anderson Jr.
SWR

Boys and girls and grownups too,
Should drink Reiss milk each day,
And build strong bones and healthy teeth,
I've heard my daddy say.

Gene Aufdenberg

When I get old,
I don't want my shoulders saggin.
I want to be tall and straight,
Like the driver on Reiss's wagon.

Carole Bishop
SWR

I'm sorry for my dolly,
She's hungry as can be;
Inside of her is sawdust,
But Reiss Dairy milk's inside of me.

Iris Black
SWR-2

If all the trees were one tree,
What a great tree that would be,
If all the pure milk were one milk,
Reiss Dairy milk it would be.

Norman Burress
SWR

All the children around the town,
Like to visit Grandma Brown.
Her cakes and cookies can't be beat,
But Reiss's milk is a special treat.

Margie Lee Campbell
SWR

Bobby is healthy,
Bobby is gay,
Bobby drinks Reiss' Dairy milk,
Every day.

Betty Sue Carter

Mary has a little lamb –
With fleece as fine as silk.
He follows Mary to the dairy,
When she goes for Reiss Milk.

Billy Carter
SWR-2

Two little sisters, Maud and Mary,
On their way to Reiss Diary,
Full of pep as they can be,
Cause they both drink Reiss's milk, you see.

Charles Edward Clinton	I dearly love my orange juice, Chocolate milk I just adore, Reiss Dairy products sure are swell, Oh, Mama, give me more.
Martha Cockrel	Sing a song of Reiss Milk Morning, noon and night It helps to brighten up the day And makes the world alright.
Ethel Cope SWR	Mary! Mary! My pretty Mary, What makes your red cheeks glow? With rest each day, and outdoor play, And REISS MILK, I know!
Gene Cope SWR	I like taters once a day, And stew about once a week, But I like Reiss' chocolate milk Every time I eat.
Jolene Corlew SWR	Early to bed, Early to rise Drink Reiss Dairy milk, Be healthy, wealthy and wise.
Evelyn Cowell SWR	Cross Patch, Draw the latch, Sit by the fire & spin. Order Reiss chocolate milk, And call your playmates in.
Doris Cunningham	You may ask your hostess For anything you like But make mine chocolate milk, Just like it comes from Reiss.
Barbara Dance	Oh, Yes, I like milk But not any grade you see, So we buy Reiss milk for it is Grade A, And so good for me.
Shirley Daugherty SWR	3 cheers for Reiss milk! Cream, butter, chocolate and cheese! They help to keep away the germs, That make you want to sneeze.

Delores Depro
SWR

Milk will make you strong and healthy,
Able to work and maybe wealthy,
Never tired never weary,
Why not buy from Reiss Dairy.

Betty Earline Drake

Come my little children,
It is time for your supper,
We have bread, We have Butter,
We have Reiss' Milk for supper."

Dale Enterline, Jr.
SWR

All the little children,
That lived in the shoe,
Drank Reiss Dairy milk,
And then they grew and grew and grew.

Mary Jane Farris

Fuzzy Wuzzy was a bear
Fuzzy Wuzzy had no hair
Fuzzy drank Reiss Dairy milk
Fuzzy's hair is smooth as silk

Mrs. W. M. Files

Pasteurized milk is the best for your child,
It will make him so lively,
You'll think he's gone wild.
For he will leap; he will hop;
And jump and play,
If you give him REISS MILK at least twice a day.

Mrs. E. F. Finck

Come my children, and let us drink REISS'S Milk for cheeks so pink,
Let us whip the heavy cream, and make desserts taste like a dream,
'Tis fun to eat, 'tis fun to play when the dairy truck stops by each day.

Mrs. E. F. Finck

It's pasteurized, it's bottled clean,
For health insurance, as you know,
And Reiss Dairy milk pays dividends
In peppy feet and cheeks aglow.

Mrs. E. F. Finck

Good, indeed, is Reiss' milk
For health insurance, as you know,
It's safe, because it's pasteurized,
Give children milk and watch them grow.

Marcella Golightly	Cinderella at the ball, Fairest maiden of them all, Rosy skin so smooth as silk, She always drinks Reiss Dairy milk.
Virginia Grimes SWR	I have a little sister, Oh how her cheeks do glow, Because at every meal, She drinks Reiss Dairy milk you know.
Shirley Jean Harper	I know a little girl that drinks Reiss milk, Her hair is curly and feels like silk. Her cheeks are rosy, her eyes are blue, She laughs and sings the whole day through.
Dorris Harschbarger SWR	Little Jack Horner sat in a corner Drinking a glass of milk His cheeks were cherry and he was merry For he drank REISS DAIRY MILK
Carol Headlee	Mary was as thin as she could be, In school her grades were "C" or "B", She drank Reiss Dairy milk each day, And now at school, she makes "Grade A".
Carol Headlee	Frail weak Tommy couldn't play, But to do so was his aim; He drank milk and now he's strong, And today he won the game.
Walter Hughes, Jr. SWR	Old Mother Hubbard still goes to her cupboard, But the cupboard is never bare, For when she opens the door, She always makes sure that Reiss Dairy milk is there.
Frances Husher SWR	I had a little pig, He didn't weigh a pound, I fed him Reiss Milk, Till his tummy dragged the ground.
Bob Husker	Not gold but only Reiss Dairy milk Can make people great and strong, So drink a pint morning, noon and nite, And live healthy all along.

Billy Joe Jenkins
SWR

Reiss Dairy milk is good for me,
It makes me sing so merrily,
It makes me happy, it makes me gay,
And that's the reason I drink it every day.

Billy Keasler
SWR

Billy, sweet as pie,
He has such pep.
It would make you sigh.
He drinks Reiss Dairy milk, that's why!

Bobby Keasler

Let Them Ration Coffee,
Let them ration tea,
Let them ration Reiss Dairy Milk,
No Sir'ree.

Billy Joe Killian
SWR – 3

I drink Reiss' milk three times a day,
It builds you up in such a logical way,
It makes you healthy, happy, and gay,
You'll like it too, so buy from your grocer every day.

Robert Dale Killian

My little baby brother and I like Reiss' milk,
I'll tell you why,
It makes us Healthy, Happy and Gay,
You'll like it too, so try it today.

Robert Dale Killian

I have a little baby brother
Whose hair is fine as silk,
And he grows stronger every day,
From drinking Reiss Milk.

Ardeth Kirby
SWR

A skinny boy moved into town,
For him I did feel sad,
So I told him about Reiss' chocolate milk,
Boy! Did he gain and is he glad!

Clyde Lee Lammers
SWR

There was a weakly boy,
Who moved into town and felt very sad,
I told him about Reiss' milk,
And now he is very glad.

Barbara Ann Lane
SWR

I am a milk bottle, I ramble all over town,
I'm full of Reiss Milk as pure as can be found,
So wash me and set me out to dry,
The driver will get me as he passes by.

Jerry Lane
SWR

If wishes were horses,
And we all could ride,
I'd drink Reiss' milk,
And race to your side.

Maxine Lane
SWR

I like to play in the daytime,
And sleep well every night,
So I drink Reiss milk at mealtime,
It makes me feel all right.

Clyde Lee Launius

There was a weakly boy,
Who moved into town and felt very sad,
I told him about Reiss' Milk,
And now is he very glad

Mrs. Matt Lewis
SWR

Reiss Dairy milk is good you see,
And brings good health to you and me,
So let us drink it all day long,
Then we can smile and sing a song.

Francis Limbaugh

If the weather makes you feel down and out,
And there's nothing you want to eat,
Just drink a glass of Reiss Milk,
It's a treat that's hard to beat.

Jeanne Maxwell

The basketball team was in such a slump,
But now their stock has taken a jump,
For filled with vigor, pep, and vim,
They play the games; they always win,
So take a tip from coach and team,
Drink Reiss Dairy milk; you'll be on the beam.

Martha McClain
SWR

Jack Spratt could eat no fat,
His wife could eat no lean,
And so between them both,
They drank REISS MILK,
And lived like King & Queen.

Faye McNabb

It's just as plain as plain can be,
That Reiss Diary milk is good for me.
I drink it morning, noon, and night,
It starts the day off right.

Susie Morris

Jack Sprat was strong and fit
For he drank milk and cream.
When it came to Reiss Dairy milk,
He left his glass quite clean.

L. T. Nickell
SWR

Reiss pasteurized milk is very healthy for you,
For tiny tots and grown-ups too,
You'll never go wrong if you think,
To buy a bottle of this wholesome drink.

Anne Belle O'Dell
SWR

I have a little brother,
Whose hair is fine as silk,
His cheeks are very rosey,
Because he drinks "Reiss Dairy" milk.

Mr. J. L. Osborn

Oh boy, what a joy
To feel as fine as silk;
Please get wise, open your eyes,
Use nothing but Reiss milk.

Katherine Parmley
SWR

I knew a little boy,
Who was very, very pale.
Since using Reiss' Dairy products,
He is now healthy and hale.

Richard Parmley

Once there was a little boy,
Whose disposition was very sad,
But since he drinks Reiss Milk,
You wouldn't want a better lad.

Billy Joe Pearson
SWR

I know a little saying,
It is not very long,
Drink Reiss Dairy milk
And you'll grow big and strong.

Billy Portloch

Little Boy Blue come blow your horn for
Reiss Dairy Milk,
Comes from good cows,
On the farm.

Mrs. Jack Powell

Come listen to my call:
"For health that is priceless to us all,
Drink REISS pasteurized milk every day,
It will certainly help keep the doctor away."

Mrs. G. Poyner	There was a crooked man, Who would have been quite straight, If every day he'd found a glass Of milk beside his plate.
Elizabeth Rogers SWR	Sing a song of six-pence, a pocket full of rye. I am going shopping and what shall I buy, A quart of Reiss' milk and a pound of butter, To take home and eat with fresh hot rolls, Oh, what a tasty supper!
Berna Dean Sikes	I don't like coffee, I don't like tea, But Reiss chocolate milk, Sure stands ace high with me.
Delcia Spiney SWR	Mom buys Reiss Dairy milk, It's pasteurized, it's homogenized, And full of Vitamins A to Z, But it's the taste and the pep it makes, That makes it Grade A with me.
Billy Summers SWR	Breathe there a man With soul so dead Who does not like Reiss milk With hot cornbread.
Pat Sutton	Red, white and blue, We all love you, And drink Reiss milk, To be strong and true.
Mrs. Gladys Terrell	Little Miss Mary is no longer contrary, Now a sweet little miss is she, She found she can be good as little girls should, If she drinks milk from Reiss Dairy.
Thelma Terry SWR	To be healthy, wealthy and wise, Drink Reiss Dairy milk and economize, At every store you can buy it, Be penny wise and try it.

<u>Golda Transue</u>	There was an old lady who lived in a shoe, She had so many babies she didn't know what to do, She gave them Reiss' Milk before they could chew, And you should see how they all grew.
Lucia Trovillion	Each breakfast I greet my wonderful treat, When the sun begins to rise, Reiss' milk each day is the very best way, To be healthy, wealthy and wise.
Mildred Vincent	A country girl come to town, And felt so bad, she couldn't get around, But after drinking Reiss Dairy milk, She just couldn't be found.
Mildred Janette Waggoner SWR	There once was a man of Calcutta, Who spoke with a terrible stutter. At breakfast he said, Give me lots of hot B-B-Bread, And plenty of Reiss Dairy B-B-Butter
Billy Bob Walker SWR	If you want to be healthy and strong, If you want the strength to play, Just drink Reiss Dairy milk, Three times a day.
Neil Curtis Whittle SWR	Jack is nimble, Jack is quick, Jack is never never sick, He drinks Reiss milk each day, To keep the aches & pains away.
<u>Mildred Vincent</u>	A country girl came to town, And felt so bad, she couldn't get around. But after drinking Reiss Dairy Milk, She just couldn't be found.
<u>Billy Bob Walker</u>	If you want to be healthy and strong, If you want the strength to play, Just drink Reiss' Dairy milk Three times a day.
<u>Mary Jane and Betty Wayne</u>	Mary Jane and Betty Wayne, two little sisters of similar name, always happy, cheerful and gay, drinking REISS milk every day.

Mary Virginia Yondell SWR	Mary had a little lamb, With fleece as white as snow, She fed it Reiss' Dairy milk, And that's what made it grow.
No author SWR	Milk that is rich and sweet Reiss Dairy is very complete. It turns out milk for which Children call, - - - - Its pasteurized, safe and good for all.
No author SWR	Yankee Doodle went to town, On a snow white charger, For every day he drank Reiss milk, He wanted to grow larger.
No author SWR	Jack and Jill went up the hill, Milk is what they went for. They drank it down without a frown, That's what milk is meant for.
No author SWR	Little Jack Horner sat in a corner, Dunking his cookies in milk, The milk disappears, he gets full to his ears, and it's safe cause it's pasteurized milk.
No author	Jack Spratt was a puny child, Who couldn't take his part, He Drank Reiss Milk a very short while, Now the "toughies" toe the mark.
No author SWR	Hi diddle diddle! The cat and the fiddle; The cow jumped over the moon, And said "Drink Reiss milk at noon."
No Author	There was a man in our town and he was wondrous wise. For the only milk he would drink Was REISS Pasteurized.
No author SWR-2	The more milk, the more Health and happiness.

No author or poem SWR	Picture of first Reiss Dairy building
<u>No author or poem</u>	The whole town's talking about Homogenized Vitamin D Milk Easy to digest
No author or poem SWR	Milk Cream Buttermilk Chocolate Milk Cottage Cheese Butter Orange Drink
No author or poem SWR	Do you know? Our driver also sells our Cream – coffee cream Chocolate milk – buttermilk Orangeade – butter.
No author or poem	I'll say it tastes better and it's easier to digest, etc.
No author or poem	Ask for our dairy products at your favorite store, etc.
No author or poem (embossed bottle with no red paint) SWR	Reiss Dairy Farm, Sikeston, Mo. Phone 2321, one pint liquid, Bottom is marked Meyer-Blanke Co.
No author or poem SWR	Small 1/2 ounce and 3/4 ounce creamers
No author or poem SWR-2	One gallon jugs with metal handle

This is my father Irwin H. Reiss who was very proud of his Uncle John Reiss and his success and accomplishments with the Reiss Dairy. Several times Dad drove his family of five from our home in Sullivan, Indiana to Sikeston, Missouri for family Thanksgiving weekends and other celebrations.

Other Dairies with Milk Bottle Poems

This summary was made primarily from listings on eBay. These pyroglaze bottles all had poems but very very few identified the author. Reiss Dairy is quite unique in that regard.

Aberdeen Dairy Products, Pueblo, CO

Annette's, Savannah, GA

Bay View Dairy, Plattsburg, NY

Beck's Dairy, York, PA

Bellview Dairy, Himrod, NY

Blossom Dairy, Charleston, WV

Boswell Dairies, Fort Worth, TX

Bowman's Dairy, West Unity, OH

Breezemont Dairy, Brookville, PA

Cal Poly Creamery, San Luis Obispo, CA

Canham Dairy, Fresno, CA

Cedar Grove Dairy, Memphis, TN

Clinton Dairy, Clinton, MI

Cloverleaf Dairy, Springfield, MO

Clover Leaf Dairy, Everett, WA

Clarkdale Dairy, Clarkdale, AZ

Clark Dale Dairy, Panguitch, UT

Columbus Milk Dealers Association, Columbus, OH

Conn's Dairy, Thomasville, GA

Crescent Dairy, Kokomo, IN

Crescent Dairy, Litchfield, MI

Denver Retail Dairymen's Association, Denver, CO

Donaldson Farms, Bath NY

Downey Dairy, Williamsport, Maryland

East End Dairy, Harrisburg, PA

Everding's Dairy, St. Louis, MO

Flint Ideal Dairy, Joliet, IL

Forest Hill Dairy, Memphis, TN

Forest Hill Dairy, Smithdale, PA

Frear Dairy, Dover, DE

French Bauer, Cincinnati, OH

Gardiner's, Garden City, KA

Geneva Valley Farms, Geneva, IL

Georgia Milk Co., Waycross, GA

Gossholme Farms, St. Johnsbury, VT

Graf's Dairy, Mobile, AL

Greenleaf Dairy, Petersburg, VA

Gruber's Dairy, Shippensville, PA

Guernsey Farms Dairy, Northville, MI

D. P. Hammond, Elmira, NY

Haskell's Dairy, Augusta, GA

Haskell Farm Dairy, Binghamton, NY

Haskell's Guernsey Milk, Augusta, GA

Hawthorn Melody Dairy, Chicago, IL

Highland Farms Dairy, Washington, DC

Hilltop Farms Dairy, Peckville, PA

Homestead Dairy, Sharpsville, PA

Kembrook Dairy, Decatur, IL

Kingsway Glen Oaks, Brooklyn, NY

Kootenay Valley Co-Op Dairy, Nelson, BC, Canada

Leake Bros. Dairy, Greenville, SC

Levengood Dairy, Pottstown, PA

Ligonier Dairy Products Co., Ligonier, PA

Linnell's Dairy Farm, Milan, NH

Locust Lane Farms, Moorestown, NJ

Lovier's Dairy, Herkimer, NY

MacKenzie Dairy Farm, Keene, NH

Meadow Brook Farms, Pottstown, PA

Meadow View Dairy, Red Lion, PA

Medosweet Farms, Kent, WA

Messer's Dairy, New London, NH

Miami County Milk Bottle Assoc., Tipp City, OH

Midwest Dairy, Cicero, IL

Midwest Dairy, Plymouth, WI

Midwest Dairy, Quincy, IL

Midwest Dairy Products, Du Quoin, IL

Mill Hall Milk Products, Mill Hall, PA

Miners Dairy, Butte, MT

Modern Dairy, Berlin, PA

New Era Dairy, Carbondale, IL

Oakhurst Dairy, Mahopac, NY

Peterson's Dairy, Plainville, CT

Proctor Creamery, Proctor, VT

Producers' Dairy, Brockton, MA

Quality Dairy, Connellsville, PA

Ritter Bros. Dairy, Rochester, NY

Roberos Dairy, Savannah, GA

Roe Dairy, Sioux City, IA

Royal Dairy, Salt Lake City, UT

Royal Dairy, Front Roya, VA

Sanitary Dairy, Alamosa, CO

Sanitary Dairy, Uniontown, PA

Schneider Dairy, Peoria, IL

Schuchardt's Dairy, Sheboygan, WI

Signor's Milk, Keeseville, NY

Snee Dairy, Brentwood, PA

Spokane Bottle Exchange, Spokane, WA

Spring Grove Dairy, Atglen, PA

Star Dairy, Galveston, TX

Statham's Dairy, Cordele, GA

Stewards, Thermopolis, WY

Sunnyhurst Dairy, Stoneham, MA

Superior Dairies, St. Augustine, FL

Supreme Dairy, Alliance, OH

Supreme Dairy, LaSalle - Peru - Oglesby, IL

Tarr Dairy, Geneva, NY

Thatcher's Dairy, Martinsburg, WV

The Farmers Co-op Dairy, Greenville, OH

Thomas Dairy, Miami, FL

Tolleston Dairy, Gary, IN

Valley View Dairy, Schafferstown, PA

Vallotton's Dairy, Valdosta, GA

Vandervoort's Dairy, Fort Worth, Texas

Wayne Creamery, Wayne, NE

Wauregan Dairy, Wauregan, CT

Wm. Weckerle & Sons, Buffalo, NY

H. P. Williams Dairy, Blairsville, PA

Weeks Dairy, Laconia, NH

HP Williams, Blairsville, PA

Yakima City Creamery, Yakima, WA

Ziegler Clover Farms, Reading, PA

Zuschlag Brothers Dairy, Greenville, PA

Other "Reiss" Dairies

Riess Dairy in St. Louis, Missouri

Gregg Riess <greggriess@gmail.com>

To: reiss_steve@yahoo.com

Dairy question – Reiss or Riess

Steve,

I understand I am a descendant of the family that owned Riess Dairy in St Louis (early 1900s). See picture attached. I noticed your book about the Sikeston-based Reiss Dairy. Do you know if they were connected somehow? Did you come across Riess Dairy in your research?

Best regards,

Stephen Reiss reiss_steve@yahoo.com

To: Gregg Riess, gregg.riess@us.gt.com

Hi, Gregg. Thanks for your email. This is fascinating. Yes, I published Reiss Dairy in 2009. The dairy founder, John Reiss, was my great uncle as the younger brother of my grandfather George Reiss. I Googled Riess Dairy as it appears in the background of your photo and got no hits. I can't imagine that Reiss Dairy would misspell their own name unless it was as a temporary joke. Our family has always been plagued with pronunciation. I grew up with it pronounced "rice" but several of my relatives have given up and go by "reese".

Steve

Stephen Reiss <reiss_steve@yahoo.com>

To: Gregg Riess, gregg.riess@us.gt.com

Hi, Gregg. I've done more checking and found Riess Land and Dairy Company in St. Louis. There is a 1917 entry where their horse and a cow were checked by the Deputy State Veterinarian for tuberculosis and passed. There is an entry on the July 2, 1910 from *The National Provisioner* saying the Riess Land and Dairy Company was incorporated with capital stock of $28,000 by G. F. Riess and others. That magazine is the official organ of the **American Meat Packers Association**.

There is a similar entry in July 1910 in the *Cold Storage and Ice Trade Journal* also saying Riess Land and Dairy Company was incorporated with $28,000 in capital stock.

I looked on eBay for Riess Land and also for Riess Dairy. There were no hits for either entry.

So, Gregg, I'm kinda concluding that **Riess Land and Dairy Company** of St. Louis and Reiss Dairy of Sikeston are not related. The St. Louis company is in the 1910/1917 timeframe where Reiss Dairy in Sikeston is about 1935/1970.

Do you have any address in St. Louis or better yet, an old Riess Dairy milk bottle?

I recently did a 23&me DNA check. They found three guaranteed second cousins which I agreed with. They also found about twenty-five third and fourth cousins, none of which I recognized. None of those were named Riess.

Thanks again for your email. Please let me know your latest thinking. Thanks,

Steve

Gregg Riess <greggriess@gmail.com>

To: Stephen Reiss

Very interesting! I don't have an address nor do I have anything else (including bottles) --- just that photo. Yes, I have performed the Google search and see the same entries that you're seeing – the creation of the business with that capital.

Just a coincidence that names similar would be in the dairy business, huh? Yes, I moved to Kansas City from St Louis in 1985. I will let you know if I find any more relevant data. Thanks so much for your quick response today – you're very kind.

Gregg Riess

Reiss Diary in Myrtle Beach, South Carolina

I bought this Myrtle Beach Reiss Dairy milk bottle and cap on eBay on November 13, 2002 which led to this email exchange with the seller, Alan Reiss:

Steve, I am curious about why you had an interest in the Reiss milk bottle. This was my grandfolk's dairy in Myrtle Beach and we have been looking for a bottle with red pyro letters for 25 years. You having the last name was surprising too. Any info would be greatly appreciated. Thanks -- Alan

I didn't save the email I sent to Alan but it would have had generalities about the Reiss Dairy in Sikeston, Missouri which you, the reader, are already familiar with at this point in our book. I did ask Alan for more background on his family and their dairy. Here is his reply:

Steve, thanks for your emails. Our family came from Michigan. The Reiss name goes back to Nat Reiss who was in show business with his wife Bertha Adams from Tustin, Michigan. He died on June 28, 1916 and is buried in the Showmen's Rest Cemetery in Chicago. We pronounce our name like "Reese". After Nat Reiss passed away, Bertha remarried to Harry Melville and continued with her carnival business until the 1930s. For years the Nat Reiss Shows wintered in Charlotte, South Carolina and Bertha would visit the Myrtle Beach area where she had a merry-go-rounds, skooters, etc. on the beach in Myrtle Beach for many, many years in addition to being with the Royal American Shows. Her son, Hershel Reiss Sr., and family moved to Myrtle Beach and bought the Kings Dairy and operated it from 1938 to 1944. The dairy was sold in 1944 to Devine Tyler.

The dairy was the supplier for the Air Force base in Myrtle Beach, Ocean Forest, Pawleys Island, North Myrtle Beach, Conway area and the area along what is now known as The Strand with deliveries to Wilmington Air Base.

The grandson, Herschel Reiss Jr. is still alive at 74, lives in Michigan, and his sister Nancy Reiss Howe is alive and lives in Dallas, Texas. The only remaining family is two great granddaughters – Jennifer Howe, a television anchor in Tampa, Florida and Allison Howe Metheny in Dallas, Texas working as a special ed teacher. She has a son Reiss Metheny along with myself Alan Reiss in Michigan at the family real estate business founded in 1947. Thanks -- Alan

I Googled Showmen's Rest and Nat Reiss Shows and found what follows:

Showmen's Rest in Forest Park, Illinois, is a 750 plot section of Woodlawn Cemetery mostly for circus performers owned by the Showmen's League of America. The first performers and show workers that were buried there are in a mass grave from when between 56 and 61 employees of the Hagenbeck-Wallace Circus were interred. They were killed in the Hammond circus train wreck on June 22, 1918, at Hessville, Indiana, (about 5 ½ miles east of Hammond, Indiana), when an empty Michigan Central Railroad troop train from Detroit, Michigan, to Chicago, Illinois, plowed into their circus train. The engineer of the troop train, Alonzo Sargent, had fallen asleep. Among the dead were Arthur Dierckx and Max Nietzborn of the "Great Dierckx Brothers" strong man act and Jennie Ward Todd of "The Flying Wards".

The Showmen's League of America, formed in 1913 with Buffalo Bill Cody as its first president, had recently selected and purchased the burial land in Woodlawn Cemetery at the intersection of Cermak Road and Des Plaines Avenue in Forest Park, Illinois, for its members. Services were held five days after the train wreck. The identity of many victims of the wreck was unknown. Most of the markers note "unidentified male" (or female). One is marked "Smiley," another "Baldy," and "4 Horse Driver."

The Showmen's Rest section of Woodlawn Cemetery is still used for burials of deceased showmen who are said to be performing now at the biggest of the Big Tops. A Memorial Day service is held at Woodlawn Cemetery every year.

Other Showmen's Rests include one at Mount Olivet Cemetery, Hugo, Oklahoma. Hugo is a winter circus home which calls itself Circus City, USA. In Miami, Florida, the largest Showmen's Rest is at Southern Memorial Park where large elephant and lion statues flank hundreds of markers commemorating circus greats and not-so-greats. Tampa, Florida's Showmen's Rest is located close to the Greater Tampa Showmen's Association near downtown.

Titus M. Reiss, Cloverdale Farms, Friedensville, Pennsylvania

Here's an internet posting from 2014 – Got Milk? Did you know that, at one time, there were at least 25 dairies in the Bethlehem area? A friend of mine has a collection of milk bottles from the following local milk vendors: Bethlehem Sanitary, Szeps, **Titus M Reiss (Friedensville),** CM Chamberlain, E.O. Biery, Clover Leaf Farms, Long's Dairy, Sunny Brook, Meyer Dairy, Suter's Dairy, F ad S Matz, Green Pond Farms, Frederick Frick (Fountain Hill), Fairview Dairy, Saucon Farms, Can Ruth Dairy, Granville E Paulus (Broadhead), Suncrest Farms, Weyhill Farms, Brookfield (Hellertown), Paulus Dairy (Butztowns), Avondale, Mowrer's, Normington's, and East End Dairy.

Titus Reiss was actually born on 10/8/1868 rather than 1858. He died on 9/29/1938.

Michael's cemetery.

TITUS M. REISS

Titus M. Reiss, 69, died Thursday at his home in Center Valley following an illness of seven months.

Born Oct. 8, 1858, in Lower Saucon Tsp, he was a son of the late William and Mary Miller Reiss.

He was engaged in farming at Friedensville and conducted a milk route in Bethlehem prior to moving eight years ago to Center Valley.

Survivors are his wife, Anna S Reiss; a daughter, Edna M., wife of William T. Headman, Center Valley; a son, H. W. Reiss, Coopersburg; 10 grandchildren. A brother, Isaac Reiss, Redington; a brother, Peter and a stepsister, Amanda Seip, preceded him in death.

The funeral will be held at 3 p.m. Sunday from the late home. Burial will be made in Union cemetery, Hellertown. He was a member of the Reformed faith.

John and Etta Reiss

John Reiss draft registration cards for World Wars I and II

Here is John Reiss in the upper right corner with his siblings and mother in 1925. Missing is their sister Katie Reiss Petry and their late father Frank who died on 12/21/1921. My grandfather

George is in the lower left with the farmer tan. The picture was taken at the Reiss family farm in St. Clair County, Illinois where all of John's generation were born in this log cabin with a dirt floor that was built by their grandfather Johann Adam Reiss in 1838. John's youngest brother Will on the far left was born in the adjacent farmhouse built in 1889. The Reiss Family Farm is now the oldest lineally owned farm in St. Clair County.

Back: William, Louie, Henry, John Reiss. Front: George, Anna Reiss, Margaret Reiss Dintelmann 1925

Etta and John below in 1938 – handsome couple

John Reiss 1940 in his office at the Reiss Dairy at 523 East Malone Street in Sikeston

John Reiss in 1949

John Reiss presenting a new car to his sales manager in 1954

Delivery truck for milk in bottles and newer truck for milk in cartons

John Reiss with all of his drivers in 1954. Jim Brase was a driver from 1951 to 1966.

Lonnie and Lillian Standley

MARRIAGE LICENSE

STATE OF MISSOURI, COUNTY OF IRON:

THIS LICENSE AUTHORIZES any Judge of a Court of Record or Justice of the Peace, or any Licensed or Ordained Preacher of the Gospel, who is a citizen of the United States, or who is a resident of and a pastor of any Church in this State, to SOLEMNIZE MARRIAGE between *Lonnie M. Standley* of *Belleview* in the County of *Iron* and State of *Missouri* who is *over* the age of twenty-one years, and *Lillian Reiss* of *Sikeston* in the County of *Scott* and State of *Missouri* who is *over* the age of ~~eighteen~~ *twenty-one* years

WITNESS my hand as Circuit Clerk and Ex-Officio Recorder of Deeds, with the seal of office hereto affixed, at my (Seal). office in Ironton, Missouri, this *28th* day of *April*, 193*4*

By *Clara Schwab* Deputy. *R. P. Whitworth* Circuit Clerk and Ex-Officio Recorder of Deeds.

STATE OF MISSOURI, COUNTY OF *Scott* ss.

This is to certify that the undersigned *Minister of the Gospel* did, at *Sikeston* in said County, on the *13th* day of *May* A. D. 193*4* unite in Marriage the above named persons. And I further certify that I am legally qualified under the laws of the State of Missouri, to solemnize Marriages.

Elbert D. Owen

The foregoing Certificate of Marriage was filed for record in my office on the *25* day of *May* A. D. 193*4*

By *Clara Schwab* Deputy. *R. P. Whitworth* Circuit Clerk and Ex-Officio Recorder of Deeds.

THE 1932 FORD V-8.

The Original

DEUCE COUPE

AMERICAN ★ Ford ★ LEGEND

Fully Authorized by
Ford Motor Company

The definitive die-cast model of Ford's first mass-produced V-8 coupe.
Precision engineered in 1:24 scale and packed with a full array of operating features.

SEASONS
GREETINGS
LONNIE   LILLIAN
JO ELLEN   KAY

Lillian and Lonnie Standley moved to Savannah, Georgia in April 1994. Their First United Methodist Church of Sikeston had a royal send-off party for them on March 6, 1994. Here are several notes from their scrapbook of that event.

Dear Lillian and Lonnie,
All day I've been thinking, thinking just of you - of the times we were together, and the things we used to do. The memories are many, and here are just a few.

I remember Kay,when she was about eight, bringing a cute little kitten names "Petunia" to Georgie -- and he still loves cats.   I often think of the fruitcakes we made together from your mother's recipe. It was the only fruit cake I ever liked.   I remember our wonderful family trips to Florida, and Lonnie's great poetry, especially the "Ballad to Old Red", and the burial ceremony.

I think of the excellent record Kay and Jim had in their four years of debating.   I was privileged to watch your two lovely daughters grow up and achieve so much.

     I've thought of so many things then------
I felt a lonely feeling as I wiped a tear away, and a little wish came stealing, that today was yesterday.

I'm sure that if George could join me we'd say -- not Goodbye but Good Luck for your future.

Love,

Emily Hale

The Sharper System

214 Kramer Drive
Sikeston, MO 63801

February 27, 1994

Integrating Technology
Into the Business Process

Telephone: 314 471-0026

Dear Mr. and Mrs. Standley,

Where to begin... You have always been a part of my life and my recollections, but some things do stand out. A *few* years ago there were those Halloween birthday parties you gave for Jo Ellen. That was always an event to which we looked forward and it forever associated Halloween parties with you. That's not to say your house was one of our favorite haunts, but it was definitely part of the fabric of our lives.

Then there were those wonderful grilled ham sandwiches at the Cow Bell. I can also remember being there for activities related to my time as a Boy Scout. I guess it was for review boards, but there was usually a treat associated with the visit.

Whenever I returned to Sikeston for a visit, seeing you was both a pleasant experience and a bit of a rudder. No matter where I went or what I did, there was always a part of Sikeston, my parents friends, and the parents of my friends that provided an added bit of stability. Mr. Standley, it was always good to see you in the choir, to see you recognized as the oldest father in the church one time, and more recently it has been my privilege to sit with you in the Chancel Choir.

We have never been close outwardly, but you two have been very close to me in many ways over the years. Some of those ways are not understood, just felt. I will miss you. God Bless and God's Speed in your journey.

With love,

Harry and Anita Sharp

Harry G. Sharp, III

Jean S. Collins

#9 Bel Air Drive
Sikeston, MO 63801
March 2, 1994

Dear Lillian and Lonnie,

When I think back to early memories of you in the forties
and fifties, the images are still clear. Lonnie was building and
managing a highly successful dairy business. The Cowbell was a
favorite of everyone. In addition he was a community leader --
school board, church responsibilities, Chamber of Commerce and
civic activities which later merited him the "Man of the Year'
designation.

Lillian was also a Girl Scout district officer, entertaining
and busy on the social scene, involved in many school activities
and doing all the fine things that good mothers and homemakers do.
I felt that you both cut quite a swathe - beautiful clothes and
cars, frequent travel to Washington D.C. on dairy business, bright
and attractive daughters who were student leaders. Sometimes you
would let them stay with Keith and me when you were away, and
always brought back lovely thank-you gifts for us.(which I still us)

Your parties were socially brilliant. Does this 1949 invitation
remind you of that wonderful Hallowe'en party when costumed guests
followed treasure hunt directions all over town, never knowing
where we would end or who would be our hosts until we finally
reached the old dairy building on Malone? Who could forget your
Country Club dinner when Lonnie invited the whole C.C. membership?
That's class! And there were the artful 16th birthday balls
for JoEllen and Kay at the Club. I still remember your creative
decorations with great globs of pink heather. Beautiful!

For 14 summers our families vacationed at the El Sabala at
Redington Beach, FL. I think of those June days on the ocean
beach, evening dinners at the Kapok Tree Inn or The Pelican in
Clearwater. The Sikes, the Hales, the Collins, the Standleys and
others all had some anxious moments when our children were growing through their teen years. These good times and rich memories
were the facric of lifelong relationships which I treasure.

Over the years we have experienced college, weddings, severe
illnesses, hospitals, funerals, grandchildren, house make-overs,
active church life. Now we are at a time when an hour's conversation over a cup of coffee seems downright special.

Others will write of the loss to church and community life
which will follow your moving away. As for me, it will be a
personal loss of friends who were always there for me - to see
that I had a ride to parties after I lost Keith, to run in with
a pan of cinnamon rolls when I was in a company pinch, to share
your dinner table with me so often when I was so alone, and who
shared deep, soul-searching conversation when either of us needed
it. So---I am saddened at your leaving Sikeston.

BUT I AM ALSO SO GLAD FOR YOU!
To take control of one's life even in the sunset years -
dream of new challenges, make big decisions with confidence,
reach out for new friends and establish a new home nearer
your children --- this does not happen often at our age.

Instead of routine days, filling in time, you will have
all of historic Savannah to explore - a gracious southern
city in a perfect climate. There will be excellent cul-
tural opportunities not avaliable here, new church experiences,
nearby oceanside resorts and best of all--closer to JoEllen
and Noel, Kay and Brad.

I admire you for your courage and for your good management
in preparing for these changes. New pleasures and new
horizons will fill your young-at-heart days. ENJOY!
A great new world is waiting for you and you might be
surprised to find how many old friends- half envious-
may travel your way.

Meanwhile, we're only a phone call away.

Love and best wishes,

Jean

From Bob and Betty Mitchell

We cannot say as much as we like about the Standleys. They have given so much of themselves to so many. We feel fortunate to have been a part of it. They have served their community and church always.

I served on the school board with Lonnie for many years. During his tenure as President, he, along with his school board members, established a philosophy that has been a part of making the Sikeston Public Schools tops in Missouri. I have the deepest respect for his knowledge of education and genuine desire to provide the best for the students. He conducted the office of President with dignity and respect.

Now - Lonnie has put more time in the Methodist Church than anyone I know. I doubt there are many caps he hasn't worn. He called us the early hours the church was burning. We watched and together with others saved the columns. Joe Wagner knew exactly who to ask to head the building committee - Lonnie. I was proud to serve as secretary of this committee. As chairman, he went to extreme lengths to keep the communication open with the congregation, avoiding influence and control by individuals to control the committee on architecture and location. In fact, he was so extreme, we had 381 1/2 meetings.

Lillian - a lovely lady - has worn many caps also. I served with Lillian in Girl Scouting. She was President of the Cotton Boll Council and served on the National Council. I always enjoyed working on Lillian's committees - everything was well planned.

We served on the United Way board. One day we were out soliciting and lacked one more call. A local bar that didn't open until 4 p.m. After 4 we walked in this bar which was just beginning to come alive. Through the darkness, the owner-barmaid looked up and saw us. She said, "What on earth are you all doing in here?" Needless to say we walked out with a check.

If you haven't guessed by now - Betty and Bob Mitchell feel fortunate to call Lillian and Lonnie Standley friends.

Dear Lillian,

We have had many good years together — with Girl Scouts and U.M.W. I have so many great memories of our times together — especially, our trips! I'll miss my "traveling buddy"! Remember our trip to the United Nations and Washington and our trek to Lincoln? And I know you remember when W.S.C.S. was changed to U.M.W. and it was our job to explain the change to everyone. I could go on and on — or maybe write a book entitled "The Adventures of Lillian and Harris" — but for now, I'll just wish you well and I'll keep looking forward to the time when we can go back to the Cornhusker Hotel and eat cheese cake!

Take care — God bless you —

Harris

Lifetime Membership Certificate

GIRL SCOUTS

This is to certify that

Lillian R. Standley

is a Lifetime Member of the Girl Scout Movement in the United States and is entitled to all the benefits of Lifetime Membership.

May 15, 1995

Date
Juliette Low, Founder

National President
Girl Scouts of the U.S.A.

Rev. Charles E. Buck, *Pastor* • Rev. Gary A. Carter, *Associate Pastor*

May 3, 1994

Mr. Lonnie Standley
125 Tibet Ave., Apt. 205B
Savannah, GA 31406

Dear Lonnie,

Sunday, April 24, was recognized as "Heritage Sunday" in the United Methodist Church.
It also was a great opportunity to recognize individuals, such as you, who have been a very
important part of the church for 50 years or more.

According to our records, you became a fifty-year confirmed member on the date indicated
on the enclosed certificate.

This certificate is just a small token of our appreciation and recognition for your faithful
service and loyalty to First Church during your 50-plus years as a member.

Affectionately Your Pastor and Friend,

Charles E. Buck

Charles E. Buck

CEB/pm

First United Methodist Church

Sikeston, Missouri

Hereby Recognizes That

Lonnie M. Standley

Completed fifty years of membership in this congregation on ___MARCH 28, 1987___, we seek to honor this achievement by expressing appreciation for years of dedication and devotion to the cause of Christ, and of faithful, loving service to His Church.

Today, on Heritage Sunday, ___APRIL 24, 1994___.

FIRST UNITED METHODIST CHURCH
1912-1968

FIRST UNITED METHODIST CHURCH
FROM 1970

___Charles E. Buck___, Pastor

_____, Chairman
Administrative Board

Sikeston Missouri Standard Democrat

Celebrations Sunday, Sept. 19, 1999

Former residents mark 65 years of married life

Mr. and Mrs. Lonnie Standley

SAVANNAH, Ga. - Lillian Reiss and Lonnie Standley were married May 13, 1934, by the Rev. E.D. Owen. The ceremony was conducted at the John J. Reiss home on the family farm, which is now a part of Sikeston.

The couple met at Southeast Missouri State University in Cape Girardeau the previous summer where both were working on baccalaureate degrees. After 65 years, they both say theirs has been a very successful marriage.

Standley was principal of Sappington Elementary School in St. Louis County when they married. Standley's father-in-law, who had a small farm-operated dairy, had visions of expanding and offered Standley part ownership in the business. Reiss Dairy in Sikeston grew to be one of the most successful businesses in the region and was sold in 1970.

Mrs. Standley was president of the Cotton Boll Girl Scout Council for six years and is the recipient of the Thanks Badge. She was also president of the Women's Civic Club and Methodist Women, from which she received special recognition for leadership, and was a member of the United Fund Board for many years.

Standley was president of the Sikeston Area Chamber of Commerce and lieutenant governor of the Missouri/Arkansas District Kiwanis Club. Education was one of his primary interests and he was a school board member for 20 years, during which time he served as president for 12 years. He was appointed to the Missouri State Commission on Higher Education and served two terms. Standley, who also served as president of the National Independent Dairy Association, is a recipient of the Silver Beaver from the Boy Scouts of America.

In 1956, the couple organized and helped sponsor the first "after-prom" party, starting a tradition that is still in existence today.

They are the parents of two daughters. Jo Florence attended Sophie Newcomb College in New Orleans and earned a bachelor of architecture degree from Tulane University. She and her husband Noel Florence live in Savannah, where she is a registered architect.

Kay attended Washington University in St. Louis, Mo., where she earned a bachelor of science degree in education, master of arts degree in education and a Ph.D in psychology. She is a practicing psychologist at Severna Park, Md.

Their grandson, Arthur Bradley Soule IV is a second year student at the Coast Guard Academy in New London, Conn.

The Standley's daughters and son-in-law recently gave a dinner at the Florence home in honor of their parents' 65th wedding anniversary. Among those attending were Mrs. Keith Collins, Mrs. Kendall Sikes and Mrs. Garwood Sharp of Sikeston.

Lonnie Standley's Accomplishments

1. Member of Cedar Grove Methodist Church South 1923 – 1935

2. Valedictorian of the senior class of Caledonia, Missouri High School 1925

3. Member Tyno Chapter DeMolay at Caledonia, Missouri 1924 – 26

4. President of Cedar Grove 4H Club 1926 – 28

5. President of Belleview Community Club 1928 – 29

6. President of the Masonic Club at S.E. Missouri Teachers' College 1933

7. Member of Gravois Farmers Club 1930 – 35

8. Member of Mosaic Masonic Lodge #351 at Belleview since 1928 to present

9. Member of Ancient and Accepted Scottish Rite at St. Louis, Missouri since 1929 to present

10. BS in Education Degree from S. E. Missouri State Teachers College 1935

11. Partner and later part owner of Reiss Dairy, Inc. 1935 – 1970

12. Member of Moolah Temple of the Shrine since 1946

13. Member of the Sikeston Kiwanis Club 1935

14. President of the Sikeston Kiwanis Club 1938

15. Board member of Missouri Delta Medical Center 1952 – 1992

16. Lieutenant Governor of Division XII of Kiwanis District Mo-Kan-Ark 1939

17. Member of Board of Stewards, Sikeston Methodist Church 1935 - 1975

18. President of Board of Stewards, Sikeston Methodist Church 1943

19. Sunday School Superintendent of Sikeston Methodist Church 1944

20. President of Sikeston Chamber of Commerce 1943

21. Member of Sikeston Board of Education 1946 – 1967

22. President of the Sikeston Board of Education 1953 – 1967

23. Chairman of the Building Committee of the First United Methodist Church 1966 – 1972

24. Trustee of Wesley United Methodist Church – Sikeston

25. Trustee of First United Methodist Church – Sikeston

26. Member of Missouri Commission on Higher Education 1963 – 1973, appointed by Gov. John Dalton, reappointed twice by Gov. Warren E. Hearnes

27. Vice-Chairman of the Missouri Commission on Higher Education 1969 – 1973

28. "Man of the Year" Sikeston Chamber of Commerce 1954

29. Scoutmaster Boy Scouts of America, Sappington #1 1930 – 1935

30. Scoutmaster Boy Scouts of America Troop 41 Sikeston 1935 – 1937

31. Silver Beaver Award, Boy Scouts of America 1954

32. Chairman of Latonka Girl Scout Camp Development Committee 1966 –1967

33. Chairman of Scott County Red Cross Blood Unit 1972 – 1974

34. Sunday School Teacher and member of the Chancel Choir at St. Lucas Evangelical Church, Sappington 1929 – 1935

35. Member of the Chancel Choir First United Methodist Church in Sikeston 1960 – 1994

36. Public School Teacher –
     i. Reddish School, Iron County, Missouri 1925/1926 and 1927/1928
     ii. Principal of Belleview, Missouri Schools 1928 – 1929
     iii. Principal of Sappington, Missouri School 1929 – 1935
     iv. Teacher Sikeston Senior High School 1970 – 1974

37. Representative of Newhard Cook & Co. 1975 – 1988

38. Sunday School teacher at First United Methodist Church, Sikeston beginning in 1935 and teaching in many departments for 40 years

39. Member of the Sikeston Community Choir from its beginning and for at least 10 years

40. Among the group of four men who established the Radio Station KMPL, First president of the corporation

41. President of the Independent Milk Processors of Missouri 1959 – 1960 with 20 members

42. President of the Missouri Milk and Ice Cream Institute 1958 with 100 members

43. President of the National Independent Dairy Association with about 600 members 1963

44. Member of the worldwide Milk Industry Foundation, speaker at their convention in Dallas, Texas November 1963

45. Chairman of Okeechobee District of Southeast Missouri Council Boy Scouts of America 1953 -- 1954

46. Chairman of the Sikeston Industrial Development Commission 1951 – 1952

47. During World War II, Scott County Chairman of the Committee for Civil Defense

48. Member of the Poplar Bluff-Sikeston District Parsonage Committee for several years when the two most recent parsonages were built for the District Superintendent of the United Methodist Churches

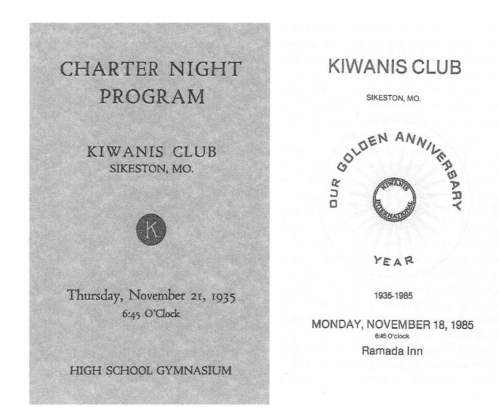

Lonnie Standley in 1952

Quality **✓** Chekd

Executive Forum

General Membership Meeting
Hotel Knickerbocker
Chicago, Illinois
November 13-14, 1956

SECOND ANNUAL MEETING

COMMITTEE CHAIRMAN

AUDITING COMMITTEE:
Harold F. Reiter, Chairman
L. M. Stanley
Fred Pearman

NOMINATING COMMITTEE:
John Sutter, Chairman
Raymond G. Colvert, Jr.
R. L. Baynton
Martin A. Willinger
E. A. Chunn

MEMBERSHIP COMMITTEE:
Les A. Perkins, Chairman
Al Loomis

CONGRESSIONAL DINNER COMMITTEE:
Richard H. Hoben, Chairman

LEGISLATIVE COMMITTEE:
J. E. Stovall, Chairman

Dairy World

March 25, 1957

Market Report—St. Louis

Milk and Ice Cream Institute Elects Standley President

Group Cites Callendar; Reid Tells of Novelty Ice Cream in Europe

By PAUL J. PIRMANN

ST. LOUIS, MO., Tuesday—L. M. Standley of Sikeston, Mo., was elected president of the Missouri Ice Cream and Milk Institute at its recent meeting in Kansas City, Mo. George Fenner of St. Joseph, was elected vice president and W. H. Reid of Columbia, secretary and treasurer.

Secretary Reid told the assembled delegates that European nations feature novelty-type ice creams, an art and business that has been on the decline in the United States in the last 20 years, he added. His conclusions were based on a trip to nine European nations for the purpose of studying milk production plants. During the sessions W. C. Callender of Johnson County was presented with a plaque for outstanding service to the institute.

SECOND ANNUAL MEETING

"There Is No Substitute
For Independent,
Competitive
Private Enterprise
As A Bedrock
For Freedom"

APRIL 12-15
1959
WILLARD HOTEL
Washington, D.C.

PROGRAM

SECOND ANNUAL MEETING

NATIONAL
INDEPENDENT
DAIRIES
ASSOCIATION

APRIL 12-15
1959
WILLARD HOTEL
Washington, D.C.

Lonnie in 1960

Franklin Reiss was a first cousin of Lonnie's because his father George and Lonnie's father-in-law John were brothers. Frank earned Bachelors, Masters, and PhD degrees from the University of Illinois where he enjoyed a distinguished 43-year career in the Agriculture Department. He would have sent Lonnie professional papers on dairy cows and various milk products.

Reiss Dairy INCORPORATED

Quality Chekd ✓ *Dairy Products*

P.O. BOX 470   SIKESTON, MO.

12-11-63

Dear Franklin,

Thanks so much for the information you sent and which was received this morning. I appreciate the fact you went to a lot of trouble, but I didn't know any other means of securing the material. Again, THANKS!

Wish all of you a Merry Christmas — and if its possible — drop in anytime during the Holidays.

Best regards,
Lonnie.

School Days Remembered

In March of 1994, Armand Moussette and Bud Bornemann were reminiscing about their school days. In the course of their conversation, the name Lonnie M. Standley came up. Mr. Standley had been their seventh and eighth grade teacher. He was also Sappington School principal.

The school had just moved into its brand new building in 1930. There were four rooms, but only three were used for classes. The enrollment was about 90 students. Miss Meyer taught first, second and third grades; Miss Cunio, fourth fifth and sixth grades; and Mr. Standley, the seventh and eighth. All three of the teachers were beginning their teaching careers. Standley stayed until 1935. The love bug bit Lonnie a year or so before and he married the charming Lillian Reiss from Sikeston, Missouri.

The young couple lived in one of the Ossing's homes at 11446 Gravois Road until the end of the 1935 school term. But their love for their old hometown overcame them and they returned to Sikeston. The Standley's fell out of sight, but not out of mind. Fifty-nine years later, Armand and Bud, along with their wives, decided to pay them a visit.

They traveled to Sikeston, found the Standley home, but to their dismay, found the house vacant. A

The Dressel family was well represented at the Standley reception. From left to right: Oliver, Armin, Selma Dressel Harris, Roy, and John.

neighbor informed them they had just moved a couple of weeks before, but she didn't know where.

The next logical place to go was the post office. They would know the new address. Sure enough, they did, but they would not divulge this confidential information. They were only doing their job.

The boys were now determined to find Mr. Standley, so Bud wrote a letter to him at his old address, knowing the Post Office would have to forward it to the new one. A roundabout way of getting there, but it worked. Mr. Standley answered the letter from Savannah, Georgia.

In the correspondence that followed, it was determined the Standley's would be in St. Louis in the latter part of June. Lonnie said he would have a free afternoon for a little get-together with

some of his old students. This leads us up to the reception held for Lonnie and his wife Lillian on June 24, 1994.

John Dressel and his wife Helen volunteered to host the party on the patio at Sunset Country Club. There were 44 guests including 26 of Standley's former students. Of note was Edna Frey Burns, a 1932 graduate of Sappington School who later taught at the same school.

Guests included Dr. James Sandfort, superintendent of Lindbergh School District; Noah Gray, former Lindbergh superintendent who also had Sikeston ties with the Standley's; and Dr. Joe Sartorius, principal of Sappington School. Dr. Sartorius presented the Society with an aerial view photograph of the school and its grounds as they (Continued on page 5)

School Days Remembered

(Continued from page 2) appear today.

To say it was a wonderful afternoon would not do it justice. The weather was pleasant, old schoolmates talked over old times, and everyone had a chance to talk to Lonnie and Lillian. Class pictures from 1929, 31, 32, 34, 35 and 41 from the Society's files were mounted on a display board for viewing. Cocktails and hor d'oeuvres added to a superb reception.

On his return to Savannah, Mr. Standley wrote a letter to Bud Bornemann which said in part:

"Many thanks for a very lovely occasion at the Country Club last Friday. Lillian and I enjoyed every minute. We met many people I had almost forgotten, but the name tags and the faces brought back many pleasant

Representing the Lindbergh School District at the Standley reception were Noah Gray, retired superintendent, Lonnie M. Standley--Sappington School Principal 1929 to 1935, and Dr. James Sandfort, current Superintendent.

memories. We were amazed at the number of persons who responded to your invitation. There can never be a repeat of this splendid party. I want to remember it the rest of my life."

Mr. Standley, the pleasure was ours. We hope you have many more years to remember it.

Photos and Obituaries

Etta Mary Reiss – Co-founder
John Jacob Reiss -- Founder
Lillian Reiss Standley – Daughter
Lonnie Maurice Standley – Co-founder and Son-in-law
Jo Ellen Standley – Granddaughter

"The Daily Standard" September 22, 1947
Etta Mary Reiss
Services Today at Baptist Church for Mrs. Reiss

Mrs. John J. Reiss, aged 63 years, died at her home 721 Sikes Avenue, early Saturday morning after a prolonged illness of carcinoma.

Funeral services were conducted at the Sikeston Baptist Church by her pastor, the Rev. E. D. Owen, at 2:30 o'clock this afternoon and interment was in Memorial Park Cemetery with Welsh service.

Mrs. Reiss, as Etta Sellards, the daughter of Mr. and Mrs. A. Sellards, was born near Fredericktown, in Madison County, November 11, 1884.

On January 24, 1910, Miss Sellards became the wife of John J. Reiss. After living for a time at Flat River and later near Matthews, Mr. and Mrs. Reiss came to Sikeston in 1910, buying a farm east of Sikeston, where Mr. Reiss established the Reiss Dairy, planted the Reiss Peach Orchard, and they became leaders in church, civic, and agricultural circles.

Two years ago, they sold their farm and moved to the present residence on Sikes Avenue. Mrs. Reiss had been a member of the Baptist Church since childhood and had always taken a lively interest in its activities.

Surviving are her husband and two daughters, Miss Audrey Reiss, now employed by the Scott County Farm Equipment Company, and Mrs. L. M. Standley, whose husband is associated with her father in the Reiss Dairy; two grandchildren, Jo Ellen and Kay Standley. Also surviving are a brother, John Sellards of Route 2 Sikeston, and a sister, Mrs. Milburn Arbaugh of Sikeston.

"The Sikeston Herald" September 5, 1957
"Bon Voyage, John J. Reiss!"

Once in a long, long time Nature brings into existence an individual endowed with a unique combination of the finest things in human nature – honest and integrity in all personal and business matters, a conception of the betterment of mankind and a sense of practicality essential to the accomplishment of that aim, the inborn industry and self-denial necessary to acquire the means to carry out a firm purpose and plan, the willingness to risk a little to do a lot, and an abiding faith and confidence in the Great Master.

Such a man was John J. Reiss, founder of the Reiss Dairy, whose loss after long illness removes one of the stalwart figures of the community who had a large share in the development of Sikeston during the years when it had its most phenomenal development. Sikestonians will long recall and regret the passage of this kindly, benevolent figure who so aptly fitted into the niche which time and circumstances made for him. Always a rarity, his type is not likely to come our way again for many years.

Mr. Reiss was one of those unusual persons who thought twice (sometimes three or four times) before he pronounced an opinion or voiced a judgment. He seldom erred in matters of judgment, but he was the first to correct his position if convinced he was wrong.

Coming to Sikeston years before the development of the dairy industry as it is today, Mr. Reiss found a somewhat primitive system of milk distribution which primarily consisted of the door-to-door delivery of bottled whole milk which had been neither pasteurized nor homogenized nor inspected for purity other than that given in a somewhat hazardous sort of way by producers conscious of their responsibility to provide a wholesome product for the market which placed so much implicit faith in them.

Mr. Reiss did a lot to change the whole picture – to stabilize, make secure and improve the local milk market. Recognizing the values inherent in the United States Standard Milk Ordinance promulgated by the Department of Agriculture, he was a pioneer in the installation of classified dairy production facilities on farms and the eventual adoption of the first Grade A rating for milk production in Scott and adjoining counties. Despite opposition up and down the line, he did yeoman service to give Sikeston and its environs the finest in dairy products. That he was successful in his principal endeavor – to give the Reiss Dairy market the finest products available – would be an understatement of facts. He set the standards from which all others have measured their service.

Lillian Standley
Tuesday, June 4, 2002

SEVERNA PARK, Md. - Lillian Zola Standley, 90, formerly of Sikeston, Mo., died at 12:45 p.m. May 30, 2002, at the Genesis of Severna Park Nursing Center.

Born Nov. 25, 1911, in Matthews, daughter of the late John Jacob and Etta Mary Sellards Reiss, she was a member of the First United Methodist Church in Sikeston. She was president of the Cotton Boll Girl Scout Council for six years and past president of the United Methodist Women's Club, member of the Order of the Eastern Star, and the Alumni Association of Southeast Missouri State University.

On May 13, 1934, in Sikeston, she married Lonnie Maurice Standley who survives of the home.

Other survivors include: two daughters, Jo Ellen Standley of Sag Harbor, N.Y., and Kay Standley of Severna Park; and one grandson, Ensign Arthur Bradley Soule IV, stationed with the U.S. Coast Guard in Kodiak, Alaska.

One sister, Audrey Reiss, preceded her in death.

A memorial service will be conducted in Sikeston at a later date.

Nunnelee Funeral Chapel of Sikeston is in charge of local arrangements.

Lonnie Standley
Sunday, August 5, 2007

SEVERNA PARK, Md. - Lonnie M. Standley, 99, died in the early morning hours of July 31, 2007, at the home of his daughter, Kay, in Severna Park.

He is survived by another daughter, Jo, of Sag Harbor, N.Y., and a grandson, Lt. A. Bradley Soule IV, USCG.

Mr. Standley was born Dec. 16, 1907, in Hendrickson, Mo., to the late Thomas L. and Emma Smart Standley. His maternal and paternal families settled in the Ozark region of Missouri in the 1820s, emigrating from Virginia and North Carolina.

After high school, he began teaching near St. Louis, in what is now the Sappington School District. He maintained friendships with his students in those years and they gathered in a St. Louis reunion in his honor two years ago.

He attended Washington University and graduated from Missouri State Teachers' College in Cape Girardeau. While he was at college in Cape Girardeau, he met Lillian Reiss of Sikeston. They were married on May 13, 1934, at her parents' home near Sikeston.

He soon partnered with his wife's father in Reiss Dairy in Sikeston, and later became president until the dairy was sold in 1970. He was president of the National Association of Dairymen,

Independent Dairies of Missouri, and the Missouri Milk and Ice Cream Institute. He was president of SEMO Broadcasting Corporation (station KMPL) from 1959 to 1963 in Sikeston.

Mr. Standley served on the Board of Education of Sikeston from 1945 to 1966, and as its president from 1953 to 1966, a period of rapid expansion of school facilities and a turbulent time in education. In 1954, the Brown vs. Topeka decision of the United States Supreme Court created an integration mandate for schools. At the first Board meeting after the Supreme Court decision, the Board, under his leadership, decided unanimously to begin immediate integration of the schools, Sikeston was the second school district in Missouri to make this decision and peaceful integration of the Sikeston schools was accomplished. The Board also began an adult education program in 1963, the second school system in Missouri to do so.

In 1963, Mr. Standley was appointed by Gov. John H. Dalton to the Missouri State Commission on Higher Education. He was reappointed twice by Gov. Warren E. Hearnes, serving until 1973, and as vice-president of the Commission from 1967 to 1973.

Active in the Boy Scouts of America from the time when he was a young Scoutmaster in Sappington, Mr. Standley was recipient of the Silver Beaver, an award that recognized his many contributions to Boy Scouting. He was a member of First United Methodist Church from 1936 until his death and was chairman of the Building Committee at the time of the construction of the present church.

As member of the Kiwanis Club for 35 years, he served as president and lieutenant governor. He was president of the Sikeston Chamber of Commerce in 1943, and selected "Man of the Year" in 1954.

In his later years in Sikeston, Mr. Standley returned to the work he loved and taught social studies at the Sikeston High School. He also became a registered stock broker with Newhard Cook & Co. of St. Louis.

In 1995, Mr. and Mrs. Standley moved to Savannah, Ga., to be near their elder daughter and her husband, Noel Secor Florence.

In 1999, they moved to Severna Park. His wife of 73 years, Lillian, died there on May 30, 2002.

Jo Ellen Standley
November 25, 2007

SAG HARBOR, N.Y. - Jo Standley, 69, of Sag Harbor, N.Y., died in the early morning hours of Nov. 25, 2007, in New York City.

She is survived by her husband, Noel Secor Florence of Sag Harbor; a sister, Kay Standley of Severna Park, Md.; and a nephew, Lt. A. Bradley Soule IV, USCG.

Ms. Standley was born Nov. 1, 1938, in Cape Girardeau, Mo, to the late Lonnie M. and Lillian Reiss Standley. She spent her early years in Sikeston, Mo. and maintained close friendships with classmates in the Sikeston High School Class of 1956.

Architecture was her passion, which she dated from watching the construction of the Reiss Dairy building in Sikeston when she was nine years old. The dairy was owned by her father and grandfather. She received a B.S. in Architecture from Tulane University in 1962. In summers, she worked with Paul Buchmueller, Sikeston architect. She received a Master of Architecture from Harvard University in 1963. She then moved to New York City where she was an architect in the firm of Curtis and Davis of New Orleans and New York.

She was involved in the design of housing projects, a correctional facility on Long Island, and the restoration of an historic hotel in Charleston, S.C. She was the lead architect of the Science Building for the State University of New York (Binghamton). She then worked with Max O. Urbahn Associates and was the lead architect on a New Jersey hospital and the award-winning Federal Home Loan Bank Building in Washington. D.C. She was also certified by the American Society of Interior Designers.

Later, Ms. Standley was on the faculties of the University of North Carolina at Charlotte and at Greensboro, and the Savannah College of Art and Design. While in Savannah, she was active in civic affairs, especially relating to architectural preservation, and she was chair of the Historic District Board of Review. She and her husband moved to New York in 2002, and at the time of her death, she was a member of the Sag Harbor Historic Preservation and Architectural Review Board.

Ms. Standley and Mr. Florence married June 1, 1992, at the Chelsea Town Hall in London, England. The location had significance because Mr. Florence's grandmother had been commissioned in the late 1890s to paint a commemorative mural in the Hall. Mr. Florence is a prominent lighting designer, and until his retirement, was vice-president of architectural lighting at Lightolier.

Lonnie with his daughters, Jo Ellen on the left and Katy plus his grandson Brad Soule.

Serendipity

Two months before this book was to be finalized, the publisher, Author House, contacted me asking whether I had permission to use the copyrighted newspaper articles. I called the "Sikeston Standard Democrat" and quickly was granted written permission to use these various articles. Two days later the phone rang and it was Scott Welton from that newspaper asking to do a phone interview about the Reiss Dairy and my upcoming book. Three days later his article appeared on the front page of the Sunday edition. I was very pleased with Scott's initiative and his article which appears below. Following his article is just some of the correspondence it generated from current and former citizens of Sikeston who have fond memories of the Reiss Dairy and the Reiss and Standley families associated with that business.

"The Sikeston Standard Democrat" April 2009

From reason to rhyme, an Illinois man's book presents the history of a Sikeston dairy. Reiss Dairy by Stephen W. Reiss of Dunlap, IL slated for release by Author House in about a month, tells the story of how the Sikeston dairy was established as well as how it came to begin printing poems on the back of its bottles – bottles that are now prized by collectors.

The story begins with Reiss' great uncle, John Reiss, who was born in 1877 on a farm in St. Clair County in Illinois just east of St. Louis. "John Reiss moved into the Sikeston area about 1917 and bought a farm," Reiss said. "He had dairy cows for his own needs but soon realized he had surplus milk." Reiss said his great uncle first started selling his farm's extra milk and then expanded by buying up the surplus produced by his neighbors to sell in embossed bottles labeled "Reiss Dairy Farm." "Those bottles are much more rare because the dairy was very small back then," Reiss said.

In 1935, John Reiss' daughter, Lillian, married Lonnie Standley who was a school teacher. "He gave up teaching school to become partners with his father-in-law at which time it became Reiss Dairy," Reiss said. It was Standley who came up with the idea to place an advertisement in The Sikeston Herald newspaper on Oct. 13, 1938, inviting "dittlers" (those who write ditties, the ad explains) and doodlers to submit their work.

The advertisement advised "Reiss Dairy will pay $1 for each ditty to be put on the reverse side of our milk bottles which were now red pyroglaze printing. The contest was a big hit although, the newspaper noted in an article a couple of weeks later, "The preponderance of ditties over the drawings submitted indicated that most folks can write better than they can draw."

Only the smallest and largest of Reiss Dairy milk bottles – baby creamer bottles and gallon jugs – did not have the poems on them, according to Reiss. "The quarts, pints and half pints all had poems," Reiss said. "If the author found his or her poem on the bottle, they could bring it back to the dairy for a 1-cent refund. Glass bottles back then were all recycled."

Ditties were printed on Reiss Dairy bottles until about 1949 "when they came out with cardboard cartons," Reiss said. "It went from glass to cardboard and the poems were discontinued." Reiss Dairy bottles from that era are now popular items for antique collectors and regularly offered at internet auction sites such as eBay. "Some of these things will go for over $200," Reiss said.

Reiss has collected examples of many of the bottles himself and, when he is not able to get the bottle, has been able to copy down the ditty in many cases. "I've listed about 65 different poems in the book," he said. "They are in alphabetical order by author." Reiss said he doesn't know exactly how many ditties appeared on the back of Reiss Dairy bottles, "but it's probably not too much more than what I've got listed." He remains interested in both the text of ditties that appeared on Reiss Dairy bottles and in acquiring the bottles themselves for his collection.

As for the dairy itself, by the early 1970s, John Reiss had died and Standley, who had reached retirement age, sold the business. While Reiss Dairy is likely to be of interest to many in the Sikeston area, the book's release was timed for the Reiss family. "In June, the family farm where John Reiss was born will be in our family 175 years and we're having a major family reunion," Reiss said. "For the purposes of that reunion, I've written four family history books. The Reiss Dairy book is number three."

"The first book is titled Quilter, Granger, Grandma, Matriarch. It is my grandmother's diary for 1949-1953," Reiss said. "It talks about life on the family farm. Her husband, George, was John Reiss' brother."

"The second book is called It Takes A Matriarch. It is 780 letters written to my great great grandmother, Margaret Reiss by her siblings, her children, her grandchildren and two friends between 1852 and 1888," Reiss said. "It covers the Civil War, a covered wagon trip to California, life in St. Louis, life on the home farm, wagon making in Davenport, Iowa, and her brother who went on two gold rushes. There are thousands of everyday life stories." Putting the second book together took about five years, Reiss said, "as most of those letters were in German."

"The fourth book is titled Granger, Quilter, Grandma, Matriarch. It is my grandmother's diary for 1944- 1949," Reiss said. "It talks about life on the family farm. Her husband, George, was John Reiss' brother."

The final book, Family, Farming and Freedom, will include professional writing and personal stories written from 1949 to 2004 by Irwin Reiss, Reiss' father.

"I will be donating a copy of each of the books to various libraries and historical societies where my family has roots," Reiss said. "So, Sikeston will be on that list."

From Harry Sharp III of Sikeston, Missouri:

Steve, all I have is pictures of bottles. I don't have any of the bottles... sorry. My former next door neighbor who now lives in California has 1 or 2.

As you saw in the footnote I put on the newspaper article, my Grandfather Felker bought the Reiss farm just a few years after Mr. Reiss sold it. When I was a kid I remember there were 2 houses and a barn on the farm. One was the primary farm house and the second looked like a rental, but I don't know if it was or not. My uncle & family moved into the farm house & I visited frequently. It had an old wall mounted telephone with the hand cranked magneto in it. There was also a small out building or perhaps 2. We used them to raise chickens at one point.

The barn had the remains of a cider press and there was an aging apple orchard on the farm. I don't believe any of the original buildings are still there. One might be but if it is, it is significantly remodeled. The barn is long gone. A lot of those changes occurred during the 30+ years I was away in the Army, a career with IBM, and some early retirement activities. I moved back here in 1993. My father died in 1994 and Mother died 3 years ago. My parents were good friend with the Standleys.

I picked my first cotton on that farm when I was pretty young. We had to get all hands in the field to get the cotton out before the weather turned.

The railroad mentioned in the deeds was the Missouri Pacific line in my youth. It is now Union Pacific and ends just east of Sikeston.

My grandfather retained part of the farm on the west end (closest to Sikeston). He donated part of it to be the local ball park, now called the VFW ballpark. It should be called Felker Field, but he never asked for the credit. It is still an active ballpark.

Golly, I started to write a couple sentences, but I sort of ran on.

Harry

From Merletta Hays Lambert of Nashville, Tennessee:

I have fond memories of the Dairy. First the name and how it was spelled.

My Daddy was working for the Dairy when I was born in 1947 until around the year 1962.

That would have been the years of 1946 until probably 1962, when I got my lasting impressions of that place.

I remember when I was about 5 year old, getting to go inside and see the cottage cheese being made, and the smell of the milk, and the wet, red brick floors. The silver shiny vats and the people Daddy worked with, Mr. Green and Mr. Wallace.

Mr. Standley his boss, I can't remember the man who had the flat top cut, red hair's name right now, was it Mr. Reiss? (I was only 5 or so but I am gifted with a vivid memory that all my friends and kin envy today.)

I remember Daddy's stiff white uniforms and that tall white cap.

I even remember that Daddy had come from Arkansas when he was a child and they sewed ARKIE on his name patch on the front of his uniform.

I wish I had that patch to keep.

I remember going into the ice cream restaurant in the front of the Dairy and sitting at the bar and feeling so rich and important.

I remember Daddy hurrying home for a big noon meal his Mom cooked for us daily, and heading back to work.

I remember her washing his uniforms in a wringer washer and then hanging them in wire pant stretchers to dry, then iron the creases sharp.

I remember walking to the Dairy just to get to ride back home with Daddy.

We lived down Gladys St. two blocks from the main highway and that felt miles away to me.

I remember Daddy brought home a trial ice cream flavor one night. It was pumpkin and I loved it, but it didn't make the cut and never was sold to the public.

I remember Daddy got to bring home the discards or misprinted quart milk cartons and he would fill them with garden vegetables and use them for freezer containers.

I remember seeing the guys at work there go to a cylinder type roller ice maker in the narrow driveway between buildings and scoop up a dipper full of shaved ice and eat it to cool off.

I remember the milk man dropping off milk and butter on our porch every morning.

I would have sleepovers with my girlfriends from South Grade School, and we would set it in our heads to play games and watch TV until the milk man came (around 5:00 a.m.) and then go to bed.

I remember that our neighbor up the street, Mr. and Mrs. Yeargain's black and white pug dog would eat our box of butter if we didn't get it off the porch real quick.

I remember Daddy had a red thin jacket with a zipper up the front and it had Reiss Dairy on the back. I wish I had that today.

AND who could forget the Cow Bell neon sign in front of the restaurant. Dark wine color and the clapper going back and forth back and forth.

I have a milk bottle from there also. The dittie on it is by Mary Virginia Yondell. It says: Mary had a little lamb with fleece as white as snow. She fed it Reiss' Dairy Milk and that's what made it grow. I am sending a photo of the bottle too.

I also have a milk "order form" receipt, price and date, and list of things ordered. I will send a photo of that to you.

Then I remember Daddy getting a 10 year gold watch from the Dairy. The ceremony was December 1956.

I have an 8x10 photo of that presentation on my bedroom wall today. I will send that picture also.

My, this BOOK announcement has sure awakened a lot of memories for this 61 year old. I know I will have more and more memories as I think about this and remember.

I want the book about the Dairy, and I also want the other two that were mentioned in the article.

I guess I should say my Daddy was James Merrill Hays. He was known there as Arkie, or J.M. or Merrill.

I am Merletta Hays Lambert and now live in Nashville, TN. I visit Sikeston often and still call that home.

I would not have known about this book or the article, if a lady from Texas, that gets the Sikeston paper, had not found this article, and just happened to send it to anyone on her email list that is from Sikeston. She had NO IDEA my Daddy had worked there.

I am hoping to hear from you and for sure get the particulars on how to get the three books when they are in circulation.

Merletta Hays Lambert

231 Downeymeade Dr.

Nashville, TN 37214

615-883-3053

kizzymert@comcast.net

From: Judy Queen <creekqueen@hotmail.com>
To: reiss_steve@yahoo.com
Sent: Friday, December 7, 2012
Subject: Milk bottles

Hi, Mr. Reiss. I am Judy Wallace Queen who grew up in Sikeston, MO, just around the corner from where the Standley's lived. Mr. John Reiss often played cards with my mother and Mr. and Mrs. Burl Heath. Mr. Reiss was a wonderful gentleman and liked very much. I also played in the Sikeston High School band with Jo Ellen. Jo was two years older and I think Kay was a year or two younger.

I now live in French Village, MO and have a younger friend (60 ish) who collects Reiss Dairy bottles. He was happy to find your name in the National Association of Milk Bottle Collectors this year. We have a lot of questions and I wonder if we might give you a call? Such as where to buy your books, how many bottles with different poems, and which ones are hard to find. His name is David Lee.

I hope you will give me a good time to call. Thanks,

Judy Queen

Reiss Dairy Book Signing in Sikeston

September 19, 2009 Saturday – Reached "The Depot" at 9:45 to set up for the book signing. Met Harry Sharp who organized this event. He was in the Sikeston High School class with Jo Ellen Standley, Katy's older sister and knew the Standley and Reiss families very well. His wife is on the board of The Depot which is indeed a very well-done museum with numerous displays about historic Sikeston. Harry has been a lay Methodist pastor for the last 20 years. We had several missions work team destinations in common including the Appalachian Service Project which my wife and I had just visited ten days earlier in Virginia.

Harry had made my book signing a formal part of the class reunion weekend so about 25 folks from the Class of 1959 showed up during our two-hour event. Another 25 or so came as former employees and friends of the Reiss Dairy. We sold 43 copies altogether including three that I traded for very rare Reiss Dairy egg cartons and one plus cash I traded for an old Reiss Dairy milk can. Best of all was the surprise appearance of our son Adam Reiss and his wife Heather who had traveled 500 miles round trip from their home in Springfield, IL. I was overwhelmed and thoroughly appreciative.

My speaker notes chronology appears below. The book signing ended at noon. Katy took us to the cemetery where her family plot includes her Reiss grandparents, her mother Lillian, and her aunt Audrey. Last June, Katy had scattered the ashes of her father Lonnie and sister Jo Ellen on his homestead in the Ozarks. Katy then took us to the Reiss Dairy built in 1949 which is now an insurance office and a travel agent office. Next she took us to the old John Reiss farm where her grandfather had first started his dairy business in 1928.

We said our goodbyes and then showed Adam and Heather the throwed rolls scene at Lamberts. It was 3:00 on a Saturday afternoon and the wait for a table was 1 hour 45 minutes!!! "Throwed rolls" has really put these guys on the map. They have branch restaurants in Ozark, Missouri and Foley, Alabama. The four of us caravanned back to Springfield, made a quick visit to their home and pets, and then enjoyed dinner together before Diane and I drove home to Dunlap outside of Peoria to arrive about 10:30.

1877 – John Reiss born

1909 – John Reiss moved to southeast Missouri at age 32

1910 – John Reiss married Etta Sellards and had two daughters, Lillian and Audry

1919 – John Reiss bought farm two miles east of Sikeston

1928 – Started Reiss Dairy Farm

1934 – Lillian Reiss married Lonnie Standley and had two daughters, Jo Ellen and Katy

1935 – Three employees, two producing farms, 90 gallons/hour, one delivery truck. Moved into Sikeston at 523 East Malone Street with 1,360 square feet. Name changed to Reiss Dairy.

1938 – October 13 advertisement for Ditties & Doodles." Would pay $1.00 if used.

1939 – Price was $.10 per quart and $.05 per bottle deposit

1942 – Sold the farm

1945 – Price was $.14 per quart and $.05 deposit

1949 – February 3 for new building, new location, and paper cartons. Jo-Kay trade name for ice cream. Cow Bell dairy bar. Location was 526 S. Main Street.

1957 – September 5 John Reiss passed away.

1970 – Reiss Dairy is sold

2009 – August 5 Lonnie Standley passed away at age 99. His favorite poem was Fuzzy Wuzzy by Mary Jane Farris.

Katy Standley in the middle, me on the right

Above is the Reiss Dairy building at 523 E. Malone in a new life as a tax prep store. Below is the Reiss Dairy building at 526 South Main Street in a new life as an insurance office.

Have poem, need bottle!!!

Reiss Dairy milk built strong bonds and strong bones.

John and Lonnie were good to family, friends, and crew,

And to Sikeston, their customers, and their homes.

May the Reiss and Standley legacies always remain true.

Lightning Source UK Ltd.
Milton Keynes UK
UKHW050244260920
370528UK00006B/121